Surfing Tsunamis of Change

Surfing
Tsunamis
of
change

A Handbook for Change Agents

by Shanah Trevenna, BSc.Mech.Eng., M.A.

Dear Vicki
Thanks for being a
Change agent for UH!
Let's stay in touch
much aloha,
Shanah

Design by Confluence Book Services

Published by Island Moonlight Publishing
PO Box 10
Mountain View, HI 96771 USA

PO Box 119
Nuhaka, 4165 New Zealand

www.IslandMoonlight.com

To contact the author, please email
shanah@surfingtsunamisofchange.com

ISBN: 978-09677253-3-8

Printed in the United States of America

For my parents, Caroline, Ken, and Melissa, who have each in their own way showed me the power of unconditional acceptance, support and love.

Table of Contents

Dedication v

Core Values for Change Agents xi

Value 1: Sustainability is Sexy xi

Value 2: Pull not Push xi

Value 3: Perspectives, not Agendas xi

Value 4: Process not Destination xi

Value 5: Beyond Us verses Them xii

Value 6: Create by Consensus xii

Value 7: Cyclic not Linear xii

Foreword xiii

Acknowledgement xvi

Preface xix

PART 1: Understanding Waves of Change 1

CHAPTER 1: A 200 Year History of Change 3

CHAPTER 2: Exploring the Futures 14

CHAPTER 3: What Suffocates Change? 19

3.1 Path Dependency 20

3.2 Risk Aversion and Liability 21

3.3 Wicked Challenges 22

3.4 Top-down Bottom-up Tension 22

PART 2: 30 Axioms for Surfing Change 27

CHAPTER 4: Bridging for Change 29

CHAPTER 5: Change Agents Unite 40

CHAPTER 6: Interactively Launching Change 52

CHAPTER 7: Growing Change 56

CHAPTER 8: Implementing Change 62

CHAPTER 9: Replicating Change 75

CHAPTER 10: Engaging Everyone 82

CHAPTER 11: Empowering the Powerless
     as Change Leaders 86

CHAPTER 12: A New Model for Change 94

PART 3: Riding the Waves.............................**101**

CHAPTER 13: The Business Case for Change..................103

CHAPTER 14: Big Change for a Preferred Future...........111

14.1 Progressive Increments for
  Cumulative Change 115

14.2 Identifying and Leveraging
  Triple Bottom Line Benefits....................119

14.3 Mobilizing Community Level Action
  to Implement Systemic Change 119

14.4 Addressing Path Dependency to
  Implement New Technologies 122

14.5 Mobilizing Change Agents 123

And So It Continues...........................125

FURTHER REFLECTIONS: Evolving Sustainability
as the Vehicle for Change.......................128

Sustainability Emerges During a Global
  Paradigm of Scarcity 130

Sustainability is Co-opted As
  Sustainable Development 132

Sustainability Positions the Economy and
  Society Against the Environment 133

Making Sustainability Useful in Real-Life Planning..134

SUSTAINABILITY AS SEVEN GUIDING PRINCIPLES...136

Principle 1: The Triple Bottom Line 139

Principle 2: Closed Loop Cycles...............................139

Principle 3: Ecological/Carbon Footprint.................139

Principle 4: Zero Waste..140

Principle 5: Zero Energy 140

Principle 6: Local First..141

Principle 7: Carrying Capacity
            and Self-Sufficiency 141

APPENDIX: Methodology for
Educational Sustainability Assessments 143

Method of Distributing Survery 144

Method of Conducting Lighting Assessment.............151

Method of Conducting Air
        Conditioning Assessment 153

Method of Conducting Plugload Assessment 154

Method of Conducting Waste Assessment 155

Method of Conducting a Water Assessment...............155

Method for Collecting Data for
        Energy Star Savings...157

Method of Educational Outreach 158

BIBLIOGRAPHY...161

ABOUT THE AUTHOR 167

Core Values for Change Agents

These values are the key to the dynamic culture of a team of change agents called the HUB (for Help Us Bridge) that made an impact on their local and statewide community. This book will share their journey and show how these values laid the foundation for a movement.

VALUE 1: Sustainability is Sexy

Sacrifice: focusing on what you don't have.
Sexy: exciting, a world of new opportunities, confidence, "beyond the norm." Sustainability as a vehicle for change is oriented toward what you gain, not lose; toward solutions, not problems; toward the positive, not the negative; toward sexy, not sacrifice.

VALUE 2: Pull not Push

Teams thrive when members work on what they love and not what they feel pushed to do. There should be an attraction to the areas of change you want to work on; you should feel drawn in and have more energy after you engage, rather than less.

VALUE 3: Perspectives not Agendas

Change is a creative collaboration that comes from many disciplines, many voices. No one needs to have it all mapped out. It's not about knowing the answers or coming with an agenda to push though; it's about working with diverse perspectives to find solutions that work. The HUB doesn't promote one viewpoint, but supports and provides forums for many viewpoints.

VALUE 4: Process not Destination

"There's so much value in just starting."
Many feel overwhelmed or fall into what we call the perfectionism vortex. There is value in just doing the best you can rather

than being perfect. A step in the right direction reveals the next step. Overarching principles guide you but you must be very fluid in the process. Keep the big picture in mind but be supple and flexible in how you get there.

VALUE 5: Beyond Us versus Them

The HUB strives to diffuse polarizations between opposing parties and viewpoints. Leaving differing beliefs intact while finding common ground and similar interests creates bridges that many think are impossible, and ultimately finds creative solutions and gets things done.

VALUE 6: Create by Consensus

The HUB respects voices of all ages, levels of interest, experience and walks of life so the big picture can come together. Our decision making process is consensus based, open and transparent.

VALUE 7: Cyclic not Linear

Linear: some outputs from a process are waste in that they don't feed into another process.

Cyclic: returning those same outputs into the next process, so waste equals food or fuel.

This applies to human interactions as well:

Linear: you know someone got linear with you when you walk away feeling drained.

Cyclic: you both walk away feeling super stoked and energized.

The goal is to recognize linear situations and make them cyclic. We can take negative energy pollution and turn it into compost for common grounds.

Foreword

By Krista Hiser
Associate Professor of English
Kapi'olani Community College
University of Hawaii

This book can be read as a narrative, a memoir, or as a case study; however, as the title suggests, it is really handbook for creating positive change in any arena. It can be read as a book about sustainability, or as a guide to cultivating leaders and the change agent skills they will bring to the future. These skills, articulated by College Student Educators International (ACPA) include: resiliency, curiosity, passion, self-awareness, tenaciousness, assertiveness, empathy, and optimism, among others.

Whenever I wonder if the change is really happening in Hawaii, and in the University of Hawaii (UH) system, I remind myself that when I started as a faculty member at Kapi'olani Community College in 2001, we did not even have recycling on campus. There were students in my English 22 class that had never heard of recycling. I remember one student commenting, "It had never occurred to me (before this class) that someone would go to a specific place to get rid of a plastic bottle." Putting campus recycling into my course curriculum was my introduction to sustainability and my first attempt at being a change agent from within my faculty position.

It took us six years to create a campus recycling program. The lessons I learned from colleagues, students, and administrators were: be patient, go slow, true change takes time.

Today, in 2010, we have biodegradable cutlery, a worm bin, multiple campus gardens, room scheduling around A/C usage, de-lamping projects, sustainability across the curriculum, and renewable energy installation right around the corner. Positive change is absolutely happening, *and it is accelerating.*

Today, every one of the UH system campuses has its own special initiatives that have brought out the best visions of students, faculty, administrators, and Facilities staff. In my opinion, we owe much of this momentum to Sustainable Saunders and the leadership of the HUB (Help Us Bridge) student group. The data that they collected was immensely helpful to others who could say, "Saunders saved $150,000 by de-lamping and reducing air conditioning. We should try that."

I met Shanah Trevenna, the coordinator of the HUB group, in 2008. I was taking a graduate course at UH called Management and Leadership, and I had an assignment to 'shadow' someone that I saw as a leader. My task was to analyze my subject's leadership style using Bolman and Deal's leadership frames: structural, human resources, symbolic, and political. I'd arranged to shadow my department chair that week, since I am trained to see those 'above' me in the system hierarchy as the leaders of the institution. But after hearing Trevenna talk about turning campus challenges into opportunities, I realized that leadership comes from all directions, and change really comes from top down, bottom up, and sideways efforts all at once.

I emailed Shanah to ask if I could follow her around. "Sure, how about tomorrow," she replied. I followed her for five hours: to an entrepreneurial networking lunch, a finance meeting, and a HUB group meeting. I interviewed two of the HUB student leaders, and turned what was supposed to be a six-page summary into a fifteen-page essay. I learned new ideas about leadership, and the paper was the beginning of a satisfying professional collaboration; I had been, as the team would put it, "hubbed."

One of the observations that has really stuck with me from the paper was about the to-do list that one of the undergraduate students left the finance meeting with.

This student, Michael, was going to visit some banks, interview another RIO leader about their group's financial structure, and do a complete investigation of the flow of money through the UH Foundation by interviewing the secretaries. Later, I asked Trevenna, "Do you really think that guy can do all that?" She looked at me like, "of course" and said, "If he can't, or if any of that becomes a push, then he'll ask for help. We never let anybody feel alone or get overwhelmed." (Hiser, 2008, p. 7)

Surfing Tsunamis of Change explains how Trevenna developed conceptual practices to empower student leaders, such as this "pull not push" dynamic (see Value 2) and the idea of moving "beyond us & them" (see Value 5). The book combines the story of her real-world experience, influential academic theories, cultural influences, and an unfolding reflection on the unique social dynamics developed by the HUB student leaders. I hope that, in the future, *Surfing Tsunamis of Change* will be read as part of the story of *how the state of Hawaii became a model and world leader in sustainability* ... and how the University of Hawaii led the way.

REFERENCES

College Student Educators International (ACPA). (n.d.) "Change Agent Abilities."

"Required to Help Create a Sustainable Future." In collaboration with the U.S. Partnership for Education for Sustainable Development. www.myacpa.org

Hiser, K. (2008). *Building Bridges to a Sustainable Future at UHM*. Unpublished.

Acknowledgments

Every time I share our story I feel hundreds of people who have been integral to this movement standing with me. Shoulder to shoulder I feel each HUB team member tuned into their passion and devoted everything they had to pioneering a new path. I thank each of you for what you taught me with your unique perspectives and adventurous spirits. I especially would like to thank Tamara for never ceasing to wow with your expansive wisdom, Vance for setting the bar of efficiency ever higher, Sean for your immaculate articulation of everything, Jeremy for making physics fun, Isao, and the other founding members: Joy, Mary, Juanita, and Norm for laying the foundation, Daniel for bringing the joy of the ride to all we do, Ivory for leading with a rare combination of depth and grace, Tamba for making order out of any chaos, Chloe for organizing hundreds every Earth Day with your heart, Mari and Carmille for distilling three years of epic journey into our web site in just three weeks, Naomi and Christina for reminding us that art is at the center of Earth, Jennifer M. for your desire and ability to understand everything, Jessica for making design and style the vehicle for the message, Amy for including us on your obvious path to save the world, and everyone for our days of surfing, skating, party throwing, event producing, seminar holding, data collecting, pot-luck eating, dancing, bursting good times.

In small and big ways, many early supporters took the time and risk of putting themselves on the line to collaborate and advocate for our efforts. I would especially like to thank Denise Konan, and David and Wendie McClain for their early leadership; the Hawaii Research Center for Futures Studies including Dr. Jim Dator, Jake, Stuart, and Aaron for making the futures, and our existence, possible; Dean Dubanoski and the Public Policy Center including Susan Chandler, David Nixon, Diane Sakai, and Sharon Mirashiro for giving us our first home; the campus engineers Blake Araki and Dan Furuya for their hard work and open door policy; UH Foundation including Leslie Lewis and Donna Tanoue for knowing our value; Roxanne Adams for endlessly providing shovels and hugs; Facilities Director Dave Hafner for his vision, and drive to implement it; the Chancellor's Office, especially Eric Crispin, for uniting the campus for change; President Greenwood for driving systemic change; all the faculty including Ira Rohter, Luciano Minerbi, Steven Meder, John Cusick, and Denise Antolini who have trail blazed sustainability curriculum for decades; Professor Makena Coffman for passionately teaching the tools we needed; Professors Krista Hiser and Debbie Halbert for being great friends and creative collaborators, and for editing this entire manuscript during the busiest time of the semester; the Urban Planning and Political Science Departments for their unlimited academic guidance; Captain Hickey, Erik Klein and the team at the U.S. Coast Guard for hiring our first interns; Randy Moore, Duane Kashiwai, and Jonathan Weintraub for hiring our next team of interns and bridging our efforts with the Hawaii Department of Education; Andy Lachman, Bonnyjean, Sodexo, Da Spot and the hundred local businesses and organizations who helped drive the sustainability movement through our ever growing annual Earth Day Sustainability Fest; Hawaii Health Guide, Divas Doing Good, Honu Guide, Nella Media Group, the Kokua Foundation, Kanu, Blue Planet Foundation, Kupu, ReUse Hawaii, Styrophobia, Hagadone Printing, the Sierra Club, Surf Rider Foundation, Net Impact, Engineers Without Borders, S.O.F.T., Cycle Manoa, REIS, HPU Global Leadership Program, Punahou Luke Center for Public Service, Sustain Hawaii, Kamakakuokalani Center for Hawaiian Studies, the Sustainability Association of Hawaii, Hawaii Community Foundation, Ulupono, the Hawaii 2050 Task Force, the Manoa Sustainability Corps, Sustainable HCC, and Sustainable Richardson for being our organizational family and ever moving the movement forward; InterIsland Solar for our first donation; 21st Century Technologies, Zurn, Energy Management Group, Island

Controls, Lighting and Engineering Integrated, Amel Technologies, Hawaii Energy Connection, Tree3s, Erik Kvam, Mark Duda, Eileen Ellis, Alex Frost, Ron Drake, Soni, Andrea, and Ganesh with GEM, Gail Suzuki-Jones, Howard Wiig and everyone at DBEDT, Peter Rosegg, Robby Alm, Corinne Change and everyone at HECO, Cat Sawai and the Board of Water Supply, Jeff Kissel and The Gas Company, Kelly, Bob, and Jenna of Pacific Bio-Diesel, Ray Starling and Hawaii Energy, Asia Yeary and the EPA, the Hawaii State Legislature, NREL, USGBC, Johnson Controls, Energy Industries, Ray Anderson and Amy Lukken from Interface Flooring, and Scott Cooney from GreenBusinessOwner.com for giving us the inspiration, support, equipment and know-how we needed; Organic Twice Shy designer Jen McCormack for helping design our logo; and my publishers, Ernie Rose and Nancy Kahalewai, for following us from the beginning and insisting our story be shared.

I would also like to thank my *hanai* (meaning adopted) parents, Dr. Nancie Caraway and now Governor Neil Abercrombie for giving me a loving home in Hawaii and showing me how to lead from the heart; my *hanai* family Louie, Clarence, and Lono for seeing this book before I did; my *hanai* sister Dani for figuratively and literally being by my side as we broke our own barriers to surf ever bigger waves; Elaina and the family dinner crew for the warmth of family and dinners; Kerry, Emily, Mandy, Aine and my beloved Toronto Trinity Bellwoods Park crew for actualizing the potential of the urban dream; Leigh, Bobbie, Silvana, Mel, Suzanne and the Vancouver crew for helping me get deeper; Stoja, Sunny, Liz, Dawn, Asia and the Hawaii Spa Day ladies for endless summer fun; Wendy and Jen B. for twenty-five years of believing with me; my entire family in Canada, especially my Grandparents Verne, Cecile, Ken, and Curly, who created a corridor of unconditional love from St. Thomas to Timmins; and finally Raina, Joe and Joceline who, in the only way that siblings can, have been surfing the tsunamis with me from the beginning.

Preface

From: Shanah Faith Trevenna <trevenna@hawaii.edu>
To: Mom, Dad, Melissa, Raina, Joceline, Grampa, Wendy, Aine
Date: Sat, Feb 27, 2010 at 8:11 AM
Subject: Surfing Tsunamis of Change

The title of my book and an apt title to our day:-). Joe and I are good, the neighbors are in good spirits and taking precautions. We're driving our cars and ourselves to higher ground so even though the phones are jammed, don't worry about us! We may temporarily lose some power, but we're together and safe and all is well.

Much love and aloha,
Shanah

That is the e-mail I sent hours after being awakened by a mysterious siren. When I first heard the wailing in my sleep I thought my alarm was annoyingly ringing on a Saturday. Then fire trucks stationed outside my door seemed a better explanation for the constant intensity. But as I sleepily looked out my window to see neighbors towing suitcases, hurrying with backpacks or clustering with concern in the street, I knew something different was happening. As the siren wailed, no one seemed to be looking in any particular direction. I joined my brother Joe on our second story lanai (the word for balcony in Hawaii) to survey the nearby ocean.

All I could see was clear, sunny skies, perfect breaking waves, and yet oddly enough, no surfers riding them. Still in my pajamas, I headed across the street into Kapiolani Park to see what I could glean from my neighbors. The situation was quickly summarized: "That's a tsunami siren and we're being evacuated." I glanced around the scene and everything gelled into context. Someone from our community board rushed to the grocery store to stock up on disaster provisions. A father of three was just returning and warned of lineups wrapping around the block. People chaotically criss-crossed the park and the street was lined with traffic. The bustling, uncharacteristic for the first light of day, finally made sense.

My concern turned into burning curiosity to find out the facts from my neighbors. Apparently, an earthquake measuring 8.8 on the Richter Scale had rocked Chile creating a Pacific tidal wave that was heading straight for Hawaii. It would hit the Big Island first with eight to ten foot waves, followed by Maui, which would see six feet of water, with our island of Oahu then getting anywhere from one to three feet. While the size of the earthquake and the persistent cry of sirens gave cause for concern, I couldn't help but think that as a surfer I'm usually excited by those wave heights, inspired to get in the water with my board … not evacuate. Yet science wasn't always accurate; what if they underestimated the magnitude of the impact? Unsure of how seriously to take the threat, I began chatting with more people to gauge their reactions.

Neighbors from the next building felt the worst that could happen was that their basement storage might get flooded. Since they couldn't remember what was in there anyway, they weren't concerned and thought it might be a good way to clear out some old junk. The power was being turned off in their building so they planned to barbeque all they had in the fridge later that day, and invited me and anyone else in the community to join in. A man standing nearby stared incredulously at their casual response, quickly excused himself and ran toward his truck piled with suitcases. Another couple strolled by in hiking shoes and backpacks, holding hands, heading to higher ground up the nearby Diamond Head crater. I was amazed by the various reactions to the exact same information. A fire truck rolled by with the megaphone blasting, "Please evacuate to higher ground immediately." Evacuate where? One neighbor said to head up the mountains. Another said to be at least on the third floor. The choice was apparently up to me.

As I eventually settled onto the highest lanai in our building fifty feet above the ocean, I began to think about the parallels between the day's tsunami warning and the huge waves of change that are happening in the bigger picture of the world today. Recessions, dwindling food and energy supplies, increased storms and rising sea levels — all are like tsunami waves in that they are potentially daunting, overwhelming, and damaging. Many perceive these issues as I experienced the warning siren while looking at the calm ocean. There is no doubt that there are legitimate issues, yet there is no observable effect in my world and hence little incentive to take action. Others hear the warning and prepare for the absolute worst scenario, become frantic and prepare for disaster at any cost. In ambiguous situations social modeling becomes a natural resource for direction.

Depending on whom I had talked with throughout the morning, my beliefs, and consequentially my behavior, had adjusted according to their level of concern. Even though everyone was privy to the same facts, many factors including personal beliefs, social influence, and real and perceived choices resulted in a full spectrum of different decisions. As I waited for the last few minutes to pass before the tsunami was expected to hit, I wondered how it would play out and who would feel that they had been right.

While many noticeable surges of water rose and fell throughout the day, ocean levels stayed manageable with no damage and the danger quietly passed. Eventually our small gathering of tsunami watchers on the fifth floor of our building breathed sighs of relief. We had spent a full afternoon with friends, pooling our food supplies to cook lunch together, swapping stories of the very few things we had thought to 'save' from our possessions. When it was over we realized this was the first time we had gathered in the years we had lived nearby and promised ourselves it wouldn't take a disaster warning to get us together again. When I returned to ground level and strolled through Waikiki, strangers were smiling and greeting each other in the streets, everyone in great spirits. There was a definite air of happiness and joviality and it seemed that despite the many choices that were made in reaction to the warning, everyone was thankful now that the danger had passed.

The reaction of my neighbors at the fifth floor gathering to the day's events parallels my vision for the future. Regardless of the size of the wave, we had prepared through the convergence of community on higher ground. While society feels vulnerable to the many challenges facing the world today, my hope is that by interconnecting our many good efforts, we can attempt to divert disaster and be all the stronger for it. Yet amongst so many paths and choices, how can we individually and collectively know what to do to ensure our desired outcome?

The day showed that one thing is clear: while we can't control the waves of change that are happening all around us, we can choose our reaction to them. And when choosing our reactions, knowing the facts proved to be just the beginning of the determining factors. The opinions of those we deemed experts, our own 'gut feelings' and belief systems, and the behaviors of those we know and trust all contributed to our decisions.

As is the case for many decision makers, social influence combined with our own perspective on change determined direction. We weighed the credibility of each person and the viability of their suggestions to inform our chosen path. Imagine if a social movement earned credibility in the eyes of decision makers, demonstrated viable options and inspired a spirit of embracing obstacles as opportunities? If such a movement were created, then it could serve as a beacon amongst the ambiguity, uncertainty and fear surrounding change — and hopefully lead the way to an outcome everyone could feel thankful for.

It was this belief in the power of community that inspired me and a handful of dedicated students to attempt to build a social movement that would begin at our campus and extend throughout Hawaii and hopefully the rest of the world. With no money, little power, many obstacles, and much resistance, we were propelled by our passion and a shared vision of our preferred future. Rather than just making demands on decision makers, we knew we had to build relationships, be of service, earn trust and demonstrate solutions. And we did just that. While this all seemed an idealistic dream years ago, we found a way to make our many small efforts add up to big change inspiring widespread replication.

Being recognized by Hawaii Business Magazine as one of five people who will shape Hawaii's future, when the Hawaii State Legislature presented us with an award of appreciation, when receiving national awards such as the American College Professional Association Sustainability Champion, and when giving keynote addresses at Harvard and other campuses around the US, I have been amazed at how our spirited projects have fostered hope and inspiration.

In writing down our story, it is my intention to inspire others who hear the warning sirens to believe that it is possible for a small group of caring people to make a significant difference. My hope is that despite how jaded, confused, hopeless or overwhelmed you may feel in the face of our daily and global challenges, you too will know that in small and big ways, you can create the change you desire and truly enjoy the process along the way. There is no perfectly repeatable path to success and this is not a book on the ten steps to a better world or a better you. It's a story where the lessons learned were not formed into stepping stones, but rather melded into a lens through which to see change. I have had the pleasure of introducing this perspective to many cohorts of students who have gone on to become innovative leaders in political, academic and business communities. When students learn they are not helpless in the face of change, they begin to perceive and experience it differently and ultimately learn how to make it work for them and their communities.

My professor and world famous Futures Studies guru, Jim Dator, PhD, earned my deepest respect when he captured the nuances of this perspective in a handful of words: "Surfing Tsunamis of Change." As a newcomer to Hawaii I was learning to surf and when I heard the following description, it focused years of philosophizing into laser-like clarity for me:

"One of the metaphors that I have used for many years to describe the magnitude of challenging forces sweeping towards us from the futures, and our abilities to control and enjoy them, is 'surfing the tsunamis of change'. Many of you are surfers, and you know what that analogy implies – the forces coming towards us are strong and relentless. We cannot stop them or run away from them. We need to study the waves carefully before we act. We need to prepare ourselves physically and psychologically for them. But then we must plunge into the water, stroke out to the waves, choose the ones we want to ride, and experience the thrill of using the power of the waves to go where we want to go with pleasure and excitement. Much like change, you cannot control a wave, but you can choose your experience of it. In fact, you have a great amount of control in choosing whether it wipes you out or propels you on the ride of your life (Dator, 2009)."

Due to their overwhelming and daunting magnitudes, recession, climate change, peak oil and other global challenges can be viewed as tsunamis of change. Using tsunamis as plural reflects their ability to magnify and perpetuate each other, or perhaps cancel each other out. Yet, as Dr. Dator explained, the goal is to surf these waves and use them as momentum to transition into the new. This metaphor provided such consistent guidance for me that I was compelled to ask Dr. Dator if I could use it as the title for this book. His response shows why countries hire this great man to help navigate their future: "Ideas are not to be coveted, but spread like seeds and allowed to grow wherever they take root."

Change is all around us and, much like aging, it helps to embrace it because: one, it's happening all the time; and two, nothing has more potential to enrich you. Whatever caused you to pick up this book, my humble hope is that you will find inspiration, concrete tools, and a feeling of community that supports you in enjoying the big changes happening in the world and in your life every day. Instead of being overwhelmed and taken down by the world's problems, you will begin to see the opportunity for restructuring and growth in the face of challenges, and effectively begin to enjoy surfing these waves of change. My preferred future echoes the sentiment I shared with my family on the day of Hawaii's tsunami warning: "We may temporarily lose some power, but we're together and safe and all is well."

PART 1
Understanding Waves of Change

CHAPTER 1

A 200 Year History
of Change

From divorce and job loss to earth quakes and oil shortages, unexpected change is everywhere, and yet little in Western society prepares us for it. Most experience change with the stigma of failure and feel isolated and ill equipped as they struggle to simply survive the transition. Yet others see how these breakdowns create necessary reconfigurations and respond by realigning their lives for greater health and wealth for themselves, their communities, and the natural world we live in.

I began my adventure into exploring change while living in the downtown core of Toronto, Canada. With recycling stations on every corner, the second best transit system in North America, true work-play-live communities and 76% of people using transit, walking, or riding their bikes to work or school every day, I was immersed in solutions that worked. When the city came out with a new strategy such as curbside compost pick-up or a towering windmill visible from all of downtown, my friends shared my excitement as we felt part of a conscious, progressive society. None of us thought of ourselves as environmentalists since our careers spanned diverse fields like computer programming, marketing, journalism, music production, film-making, engineering, acting, business, graphic design, architecture and real estate. We didn't think of these advances as saving the planet, but thought they simply reflected the culture of our city as a much loved, thriving and growing modern metropolis. We were proud of our city, felt cared for by its planning, and felt like we were part of something great. It wasn't until I decided to take a course to brush up on the latest advances in my field of engineering that I came to see that Toronto's efforts were in response to some big global challenges, and that the successes of our city were beyond most, yet still so far from where we needed to be.

Professor Vanderburg's course was called 'Technology, Society and the Environment' and I was drawn to it since academia so rarely attempts to bridge these seemingly mutually exclusive spheres of study. On my first day at the University of Toronto before we even began the course content, I felt a door open to an entirely new way of thinking when the professor began his introduction. An electrical engineer by training, his career had begun with nearly a decade of working for various corporations, much as I had at that point in my life. Yet like me, he was troubled to see how much people suffered, unsatisfied in their jobs, even though they had all that society seemed to prize. We shared other concerns, such as the disparity between regions in the world, which I had often experienced in traveling and working in developing nations.

Here was a man who shared the sensitive perspective I had always felt alone in, and he not only felt it, he had done something about it. He had returned to university and ultimately received his Ph.D. in a field many would have assumed was the polar opposite of engineering: sociology. When he became a professor, he designed his courses to show that technical and sociological disciplines were intimately intertwined, and that by understanding their interconnected nature, we could navigate toward a more fulfilling, efficient, prosperous society. This man was a visionary, which seemed all the more profound to me when he shared that despite his highly trained ability to navigate the world, he was completely and utterly blind.

Professor Vanderburg began our journey just before the industrial revolution when families lived, worked and played together in close physical proximity to each other. While modern families ship off younger, older, and ill members to be taken care of by institutions such as schools, elderly homes and hospitals, this was not the case in pre-industrial times. There was no separation of family and work life since people worked from their houses in such roles as weavers, blacksmiths, and bakers. Home life included apprenticing with your parents or neighbors, taking care of aging grandparents or younger siblings, socializing, cooking, tending to the sick, cleaning, and playing. These many activities of life were integrated thus there was little need for societal institutions since the family, home and neighbors could address everyone's needs. This all changed with the introduction of a revolutionary technology called the loom.

In the textile industry of England at the turn of the 1800s, using a machine to weave cloth was as revolutionary as teleportation might seem today. It changed everything. It might seem that just one small part of society, those who had previously hand-woven fabric, would be affected by this new capability. Yet the ripple effect demonstrated the far-reaching societal implications of this new technology. All of the process steps leading up to the loom had to ramp up through mechanization in order to keep up with the loom's demand for inputs. With so much fabric rapidly being produced, everything downstream made from the fabric also increased.

Centralized factories for different steps in the process became necessary to maximize production. For the first time, work was separated from home life as people set out to live in polluted, crowded cities to work twelve to twenty hours each day. In addition to the unhealthy working and living conditions associated with factory life, the segregation of the many roles the home had once served left people disconnected from everything that had once nurtured them. They were treated as machines of production — their health, happiness, spirituality, sensuality, relationships and all that makes people human were of little concern to production processes. Not only had technology transformed production, society itself had become mechanized.

While these dehumanizing roots of mass production may seem archaic compared to modern society, my experiences as a manufacturing engineer for one multinational corporation had shown me that rather than move beyond mechanistic society, some companies had perfected and propagated it. While many companies now promote social responsibility and have realigned to be champions of change, this was not the mainstream corporate profile of most organizations I knew of upon graduating. From the car and truck manufacturing plants in my small hometown to the computer manufacturing company I worked for in Toronto, I didn't have to look hard to find people who felt like cogs in a corporate wheel. Given temporary entry positions where they had to repeatedly prove themselves not only to advance, but also to simply keep their jobs, many people felt like property and tools of production rather than valued contributors.

I repeatedly witnessed employees push aside the needs of their children, families, or health, including any balancing, creative or fun activities, in order to perfect, perform, or produce for their employer. In this setting the segregation of the multifaceted roles of individuals and the home had only magnified and been compensated for by inefficient institutions and the whole mess had become culturally entrenched. While on paper people claimed success at having accomplished society's prized goal of gainful employment, I consistently saw needless suffering from the lack of cohesion of the self and the home, which had become a socially accepted norm of modern society. And we had not only perfected this distorted way of living, we had successfully made it our primary export in the form of globalization.

Simply stated, globalization refers to the reduction and removal of barriers between national borders in order to facilitate the flow of goods, capital, services and labor. While Professor Vanderburg's narrative on the industrial revolution finally shed light on the shades of suffering I had seen infused in everyday life, his introduction to the concept of globalization addressed the very scenario that had ultimately caused me to quit my first professional job with the intent of leaving my entire profession for good. Because I felt my experience was an isolated incident, I had never really discussed it with anyone. Now it became clear to me that it had actually been a textbook case of how some multinational organizations had taken advantage of globalization.

Upon graduating in mechanical engineering from the University of Western Ontario in 1998, I was one of the few and the proud — an engineer with a job with a highly respected high-tech company. My initial assignment was to lead the first ever transfer of computer manufacturing production from our plant in Canada to another country, in this case Mexico. Our team in Toronto held weekly conference calls with the Mexican team as we guided them through a hefty checklist of activities in preparation for the new production. After months of coordinating, I arrived in Mexico with four weeks to finalize the details before our new manufacturing line went live. As I toured the plant my surprise and dismay steadily grew as I learned that, despite their reports of progress, nothing on the checklist had actually been implemented. Not one thing.

I quickly came to realize that only two engineers were attempting to do what would have required a dozen in Canada. The exhausted duo had been instructed by their management to lie and report that they were completing the assigned list of activities so as not to lose the account with our company. When

I looked into their strained, bloodshot eyes I knew that I had to get to the bottom of this.

It took days to locate the senior executives since they rarely set foot in the plant and seemed to spend most of their time poolside at their rented mansions or throwing elaborate parties. I was finally able to track down the vice-president for a lunch meeting where I asked why we had been set up to fail. His response was that this was "low cost geography" where we were expected to produce more for less.

"At the cost of people's health!?" I couldn't help but ask.

Surprised that his explanation wasn't sufficient, he seemed to think for a moment and added, "We simply don't have money to pay more engineers."

I nodded slowly. "How much is an engineer's salary?" I asked.

"Twelve thousand dollars," he answered with a shrug.

I held his eyes, nodding. "Well, here is last month's expense report for the two executives stationed here. Not including their rented houses and vehicles, their entertainment alone was $24,000. It seems if there were a few less parties we could have about twenty-four more engineers this year."

He paused and finally met my unwavering eyes. To my surprise, as this understanding set in, he admitted, "You're right." And then to my even greater surprise he added, "But no one is going to do anything about it."

I couldn't help my response: "Well then, #@$%& this."

As that was a few years before Naomi Klein's groundbreaking book *No Logo* brought the issues of globalization to the masses, I did not realize that I had just experienced a textbook case. While all companies are not created equal and there are certainly multinational companies practicing great global social responsibility, this is not always the case. Had Klein documented the failed promises of some multinationals a few years earlier I would have had some understanding of my experience. As it were, I felt alone without realizing that this kind of exploitation was occurring all over the world as developing countries desperate to industrialize were handing over their natural and human capital.

I returned to Canada determined to address this challenge, but had no idea where to turn with the words 'no one is going to do anything about it' sounding in my head. I finally found one manager whose work seemed to provide a tangible solution. He was developing an equation that would take into account the complexity of a manufacturing process, and to identify the number of engineers required for a project rather than rely on arbitrary assignments from executives who may just be trying to line their pockets. I jumped onto his team driven by the memory of my exhausted engineering friends in Mexico. All I could hope was that this solution would ensure future projects would be fairly staffed, no matter where they occurred in the world. I knew once the equation had been finalized and had momentum, I would have done all that I could do.

So I left my salary, cushy expense account and corporate security to pursue one burning question: How does change get implemented? I moved to Vancouver and treated the whole city like an educational center. I attended community planning sessions, legislative hearings and public lectures. I had lunches with the people I met, learned about their jobs, interests and worries that inspired them to engage in change. I took night classes in courses like Physics, Energy and the Environment, Sustainable Community Development, and Economic Development. I quickly came to realize that most of the technical solutions to the world's problems exist. From renewable energy to effective policies we have the mechanisms to create economic, environmental and societal prosperity. Yet one question remained unanswered: if all these pieces to the puzzle exist, why aren't they being assembled into a picture of something better — especially when so many seem to desire a brighter existence?

When I realized that going to class and researching these questions were just as exciting to me as playing soccer, snowboarding or spending time with friends, I knew I had found my passion. I decided that academia would be the best place for me to explore my ever-growing need to understand change. Eventually as a professor I could perhaps learn and teach about these issues for the rest of my life. That seemed to offer me the most powerful potential to learn and grow, as well as create an impact. While I felt like a house was burning and all I had was a teacup full of water to put it out, I pondered the ability to connect with an entire academic and extended community as well as cohorts of students over the years. This gave me the idea that thousands of teacups together could possibly douse some flames after all.

I literally scanned the world looking for the place where I could spend the rest of my life learning, implementing, inventing, and modeling solutions that could possibly be replicated throughout the world. I explored the idea of immersing myself in such environmentally conscious regions as Sweden or California. I actually first considered Hawaii because I thought that since it was comprised of islands with the most remote population center on Earth, it would be the model for conscious living. Without knowing my interest, a friend happened to lend me a book called *Hawaiian Elders Speak*, by M. J. Harden, which sealed the deal for me. It contained stories of remarkable people with such deep values that I was inspired to believe Hawaii had what the world needed: a diverse multicultural, accepting, warm society integrated with rich natural surroundings and grounded in indigenous values. Part of the US economy, solutions in Hawaii could perhaps be replicated throughout the most consuming and polluting country in the world. Yet its strategic location would allow it to serve as a model that could influence both the eastern and western hemispheres. Hawaii was like a beacon to me and without knowing a single person living there I went to check it out.

Like anyone who scratches beyond the surface of the typical tourist's package, I found that Hawaii had many surprises in store. The native Hawaiian influence and deep community fabric were even stronger than I had hoped. Most conferences and public events began with a Hawaiian prayer or chant and when meetings ended, everyone hugged each other warmly. When I found myself hugging a Senator at the State Capitol building after my first public meeting, I knew I was somewhere special. Yet, the near complete absence of recycling and overwhelming dependence on imported food and fossil fuel were shockingly disappointing. Hawaii paid the highest energy prices in the country to burn oil for electricity and only a small percent of the state's total energy needs came from the inexhaustible sun, wind and ocean energy that was everywhere. There was so much potential that had barely been scratched that a new path emerged for me — to be part of the evolution.

When I first met with professors at the University of Hawaii (UH) to discuss my intentions, I was told to run in the other direction. A state agency leader pointed at his hair and said he attributed every grey strand to decades of trying to implement much needed change at the UH Manoa (UHM), the flagship campus of the UH system, without success. Another was leaving after fruitless efforts to make any progress for change. Many told me that campus politics and turf wars would eat me alive. Yet so many people I approached made time for me, were willing to express their challenges and concerns, invited me to lunches and backyard barbeques and shared their thoughts, studies, solutions — anything they thought might be helpful.

Amongst the frustration, doubt, and disappointment after decades of resistance to change, there was also an undying spirit of community, belief, vision, and support. Amongst so many diverse stakeholders, there was surprising unity in a shared vision and desire for energy and food self-sufficiency, minimizing of waste, conservation of water and natural resources, and diversification for a strong, local economy. Through the actualization of its great potential, Hawaii could be what the world needed … a model for positive change.

I discovered that Hawaii is not simply the tourist paradise portrayed by advertising agencies. It is in every way a true microcosm of the world where all the political, environmental, and social challenges, as well as opportunities for solutions, exist in a magnified way. The deep and intricate interconnections of people and organizations lead to only a few degrees of separation. As is often said, "it's a small island" where tolerance, acceptance, and accountability are essential in everyday and professional life. I knew it wouldn't be easy, but it would be real. And so many shared the same inspiring vision! Nearly everyone I met knew Hawaii had the potential to be a highly recognized and inspiring model for the world. That this potential might be actualized and that I might be a participant were both considerably doubtful. Yet I knew I would go forward — not because it was probable but because it was possible. As I scientist I would continue with the hypothesis that I could contribute to this shared vision becoming a reality until proven otherwise. I dedicated myself to giving everything I had to learn from and contribute to Hawaii.

When I showed up at UH ready to explore my question of how to implement change, I was one unknown student among tens of thousands. The vision for Hawaii that inspired me seemed such a shot in the dark compared to the current conditions and trajectory. I was about to devote the next few years of my life to a path that led to a future transformatively different from anything that currently existed. While I knew it was a future worth investing in, was it even realistic? This seemed a rhetorical question until I discovered that there was an entire academic and applied field devoted to exactly what I was contemplating — studying the future!

Never having heard of Futures Studies, I was blown away when I learned that one of the world's Futures gurus who had pioneered the area forty years ago was alive and well and a professor at the University of Hawaii. I headed straight to his office expecting a long process for getting an appointment, and instead found him opening a package like a kid at Christmas. With a wide smile Professor James Allen Dator welcomed me to sit down and openly shared his treasure. It was a copy of his latest authored book and it was the first time he was seeing it in print. I knew I had found my first mentor when I saw the title: *Fairness, Globalization, and Public Institutions*. Hence began my journey into the world of Futures Studies where the transformative future I was devoted to was entirely possible.

CHAPTER 2

Exploring the Futures

Futures Studies does not believe in examining the future because simply it does not exist. Instead it strives to explore various scenarios of the future. Contrary to my expectations, I learned that Futures Studies does not promote predictions, but rather emphasizes the reality of many "alternative futures" rather than a single "THE future." (Dator, *The Future Lies Behind!*, 1998). Rather than a straight, determinate river, the future is an open delta where many paths are available. As Futurist Dr. James Dator describes, "The future is fundamentally plural and open— an arena of possibilities, and not of discernible inevitabilities." (Dator, *The Future Lies Behind!*, 1998).

Most visions of the future assume an extrapolation of currently understood trends, yet Futures Studies provides a proven framework that expands this narrow view into a more useful and realistic perception of all that the future can be. The idea is to expand thoughts of the future to many possibilities, hence the concept of Futures with an 's'. Once people expand their perceptions and images of the future, they can explore each, deciding what they like and don't like, to ultimately design their preferred future, which is built from desirable aspects, or in response to undesirable aspects of the many possibilities.

This methodology that had been used to help organizations and entire countries create their preferred future for decades excited me. Yet how many potential futures should be explored to be useful? How reasonable was the preferred future I kept hearing about from all corners of Hawaii that included energy and food self-sufficiency, mininal resource use and zero waste? Again, Futures Studies had the answers.

Over many years of study, Dator determined that most visions of the future fall into one of four categorizes he calls generic futures as described below (Dator, *The Future Lies Behind!*, 1998):

1. **Continuation** – The most common scenario where current trends are extrapolated and continue on as business as usual or status quo.

2. **Collapse** – Current conditions become non-functional as in post-apocalyptic visions, plunging society into crisis.

3. **Disciplined** – Society is conscious of its direction and makes a comprehensive effort to control the outcome, usually organized around an overarching ideology such as conservation.

4. **Transformational** – New technology, policy, and cultural norms are created, fostered and implemented on such a scale that the existing norms are completely replaced and new beliefs, behaviors and organizations are formed as a result. The introduction of the loom which launched industrial society and the invention of the automobile are both excellent examples.

If scenarios in each category are developed from these varied alternatives, a more realistic, diverse landscape of possibilities takes shape. I realized my preferred vision represented a combination of disciplined and transformative futures. A concerted effort would be required to change course, and the outcome, Hawaii as a world model for positive change, would be greatly different from the current conditions. Often my preferred future was viewed as utopian, impossible or idealistic, while continued growth or collapse were touted as the only 'realistic' possibilities. Through many conversations I came to realize that all too often, scenarios that individuals and organizations create are not truly alternative possibilities and are simply a reconfiguration of what already exists. I couldn't help but ask myself, why do extrapolations of the known win out as more realistic for so many people? Why do most visions of the future assume a continuation of the existing path?

It seemed straightforward that where business is concerned, continued growth is the preferred future of choice so investors and stakeholders can continually increase profits. I still remained curious as to why academics seemed more likely than most to consider a future of collapse? Since academics are not economically bound in their views, it would be reasonable for them to contemplate a future other than continued growth, but why collapse? A landmark paper published in 1968 called *The Tragedy of the Commons* by Garrett Hardin helped me to understand a simplified difference between market players and those outside the market (Hardin, 1968, p. 1243). In societies where land is owned communally, the 'tragedy of the commons' occurs when individuals take for their own benefit without restriction from common resources (Yandle, Vijayaraghavan, & Bhattarai, 2002, p. 4). For example, if I am a sheep farmer and have access to a common field I profit more from allowing five rather than just one sheep to graze. So I let them loose and strive to increase my flock without thought of the field. Of course the tragedy occurs when

everyone does this and there is no more field left for anyone —
hence collapse.

From my experience, market players view the future as an
endless field, while those outside the market tend to see the limits
and warn of collapse. While academics are trained to be critical
thinkers and to view the big picture without bias, it doesn't serve
the traditional market to consider the overall conditions of the
commons. Thus, many professors when critiquing the status quo
tend to deconstruct toward collapse as they feel it is their duty to
share the 'writing on the wall' based on the known facts. While
their wake up call is often warranted considering the current
trajectory, it is rarely linked to creative solutions beyond existing circumstances. So if business favors continued growth and
academics describe collapse, who is focusing on a disciplined or
transformative future?

Interestingly, I have most often found the arena of disciplined
futures to be led by government. From a simplified perspective,
policy can be considered an attempt at societal discipline. I rarely
see policies as transformational since politicians often do not want
to risk putting themselves in opposition to status quo, since popular
vote is what keeps them in power. As such, there are few institutions, organizations or groups striving for a transformative future.
But a transformative future is exactly what I wanted to work for.
While I had worked in business that valued continued growth
and on governmental policy that attempted discipline, I desired
transformation. Yet I was now just a student, existing on the lowest
rung of the ladder at the institution I wished to help evolve.

In my first few months in Hawaii I remember saying to a
friend that I usually had a lot of money and little time, or a lot of
time and little money, yet now I found myself with little money
and nearly no time. He responded, "That's called being a student."
Additionally, I knew few people and I had absolutely no power.
And the problems certainly seemed insurmountable. Progress
had been stalled for decades and no one had put a finger on

the roadblock. While the preferred collective vision seemed clear, and now because of Futures Studies, entirely possible, I needed to understand what exactly was working against the change needed to get us there. Before I could even begin to think about what the steps should be or how I could possibly participate in the process, I needed to understand what exactly the problem was.

CHAPTER 3

What Suffocates Change?

When facing the challenge of making systemic change at the UH that would hopefully inspire Hawaii, the task understandably seemed daunting. There were so many stakeholders, massive comprehensive change desired and needed, and decades of resistance to comprehend. Needing direction I started asking around on campus and again found my source for answers in another area of study I had never heard of, Urban and Regional Planning. I was so intrigued by the concept of designing the built environment for the complex future of an entire city that, after taking all the Futures courses the UH had to offer, I transferred departments to pursue a Masters degree in Urban and Regional Planning.

The history of Planning had a lot to offer since it had worked with multiple stakeholders in real life challenges for over a hundred years (Christensen, 1985). Throughout my studies, four of the lessons learned by the Planning profession jumped out at me as useful, concrete explanations of what suffocates and creates resistance to change.

3.1 PATH DEPENDENCY

Path dependency explains how the set of decisions one faces for any given circumstance is limited by decisions one has made in the past, or why the same path is chosen even in the face of better options. For example, Hawaii's current energy landscape encompasses many 'path dependent' approaches that have combined to entrench our reliance on burning imported fossil fuel for electricity, rather than transition to renewable energy, which is abundant and would liberate Hawaii to energy independence. Why has Hawaii through so many planning processes chosen the same, less desirable, path over and over? For the same reason I am typing on this keyboard.

The QWERTY keyboard (named for the keys along the top left row of a traditional keyboard) is surprisingly not the most efficient configuration possible. Over many decades much more efficient arrangements, such as allowing popular words to be more easily typed by placing their letters intuitively on the keys, have been created and proven much more useful. In fact, the QWERTY keyboard was actually designed to slow down typists! Early keys would jam if they were hammered too quickly. So the keyboard that is the tool of Western industry, academia and government was built with the goal of inefficiency!

So why has the QWERTY keyboard remained popular when much more user-friendly options are available? Like many existing technologies saturated in their use by society, the interconnectedness of production and demand in the hundred-year history of the typewriter market created "self-reinforcing" processes that keep QWERTY entrenched (Kelly, Cashore, Bernstein, & Auld, 2009, p. 14). For example, every company that chose to buy QWERTY typewriters served to increase the incentive for typists to learn QWERTY and the more typists that knew QWERTY, the greater the incentive for firms to use those typewriters (Kelly, Cashore, Bernstein, & Auld, 2009, p. 17). The concept of path dependency shows why there is great incentive for existing processes to stay in place even in the face of better options.

If we were to make change on campus, we would have to find a way of recognizing path dependency and working with it somehow. And I soon learned that one of the strongest areas of path dependency, which seemed to permeate most conversations and decisions, would also have to be addressed: risk aversion.

3.2 Risk Aversion and Liability

I had come to understand from my many academic and professional mentors that liability was at the root of many risk-averse decisions. Risk aversion was even higher in Hawaii since failed businesses or tarnished reputations have nowhere to go to start over. As a small population center of just over one million living in the most remote location on Earth, many residents prefer to err on the tried and true path. Pierre Omidiar, founder of E-bay and a resident in Hawaii, summed up this aspect of local culture at a UH presentation. He sited risk aversion as Hawaii's greatest barrier to greatness. He recounted how in San Francisco he always asked potential partners to list their failures. If they had none to share he was discouraged from working with them since they hadn't learned anything.

So why don't more individuals and organization view mistakes as lessons? Besides fear of cultural or social repercussions, there is also the very real concern over liability. It is often perceived that doing things as they have always been done will not create lawsuits. When contemplating a green roof on campus or a building mounted wind turbine the preference of campus planners would be to avoid these at all costs as they picture collapsing ceilings and tumbling turbines. If we were going to make any headway on campus, we had to address risk aversion path dependency, especially where it might create liability.

3.3 WICKED CHALLENGES

Urban Planning also introduced a way of categorizing many of society's current issues such as our dependence on fossil fuel and resulting problems such as climate change as 'wicked.' A 1973 article by urban planners Rittel and Webber identified 'wicked problems' as those lacking simplistic, straightforward planning responses (Kelly, Cashore, Bernstein, & Auld, 2009, p. 6).

For example, creating green house gases depends on many factors including population, economic activity, the price of energy, availability of energy, technological advances, development of alternative sources of energy, government policies, world political stability, and public attitude (McFarland, Hunt, & Campbell, 2001, p. 3-13). With incomplete data the future influence of technological innovation and demand is difficult to foresee and incorporate into planning (Graefe, 2009, p. 11). Since these factors are unpredictable as well as inter-related, they represent the complexity and uncertain nature of 'wicked' problems that seem insurmountable (McFarland, Hunt, & Campbell, 2001, p. 3-13).

The challenge of evolving our huge multifaceted campus certainly seemed 'wicked,' meaning we would have to ensure the unpredictable could be incorporated, and we would have to become very comfortable with uncertainty.

3.4 TOP-DOWN BOTTOM-UP TENSION

Top-down and bottom-up tension is best described by a story from Planning that began in the early 1930s in a Manhattan that was struggling to recover from the Depression. Enter an urban planner who was sophisticated, stately and sincerely believed he could rationally restructure society for human betterment. Robert Moses was the dominant figure in reshaping the built environment of New York City and New York State for more than three decades. Moses was one of the most powerful men in New York and, although he never held political office, mayors and governors feared to defy him (Callahan & Ikeda, 2004, p. 254).

Moses was esteemed for holding a comprehensive vision of how to reshape one of the most heavily populated and densely congested metropolitan regions of the world. His decisions were driven by his desire to wash away all traces of the old and replace them with a completely new and all-embracing system. While he created many of New York's public works from Shea Stadium and the World's Fair Grounds to the Triborough Bridge and Long Island Expressway, he did so at the cost of existing infrastructure and neighborhoods (Callahan & Ikeda, 2004, p. 254). He perfectly characterized the earliest planners, called Rational Planners, who were considered experts and dictated the direction of planning with little to no community participation. While he held a grand vision of society's future that would affect a great many individuals, he did not take into consideration those people's own plans and dreams (Callahan & Ikeda, 2004, p. 255).

His letters contained telling phrases such as "you can't make an omelet without breaking eggs," and "if the end doesn't justify the means, what does?" For example, with one piece of masterfully crafted legislature he gained the power to seize any amount of Long Island property he desired to implement his master plan (Callahan & Ikeda, 2004, p. 256). And while choosing the route for the Northern State Parkway he shifted his plan to avoid the land of wealthy estate owners and instead laid asphalt through the most fertile soil of a struggling farmer who had no money or power to resist the destruction of his farm (Callahan & Ikeda, 2004, p. 257).

So what changed to sprout a new path? A critical view of the dictatorial role of planning came in a book released in 1961 by New York grassroots organizer and community activist, Jane Jacobs, titled *The Death and Life of Great American Cities*. Jacobs clearly stated her love for urban density and city life, as well as her contempt for the rigid rules of the planning theory of Rational Planners like Robert Moses. Where Moses said there was urban decay that needed to be leveled and rebuilt, she found thriving, interconnected communities worth protecting. Jacobs documented how Moses had killed a number of neighborhoods with highway construction that cut through communities creating 'border vacuums' people did not want to, or could not, venture across where entire areas were rendered lifeless since. (Callahan & Ikeda, 2004, p. 259).

Jacobs pointed out that the traffic alleviation intended by Moses' decisions was not even achieved since an unintended consequence of his new highways was an increased amount of driving (Callahan & Ikeda, 2004, p. 260). Moses justified decisions on empirical numbers such as private holdings of residents while Jacobs showed that the real wealth of most residents in lively but poor neighborhoods came from informal public networks participating in school and church activities, being a good neighbor, and keeping an eye on the street (Callahan & Ikeda, 2004, p. 259). While Moses felt justified in bulldozing many poor communities deemed 'slums,' Jacobs fought to make the voices of communities and neighborhoods heard.

While the polarization in this classic example characterized an extreme scenario, understanding these top-down and bottom-up perspectives helped me interpret the less extreme but still palatable tension between the top-down efforts of the Facilities department and the bottom-up perception of the campus community. As on many campuses across the country, various Vice-Chancellors and heads of Facilities were ultimately accountable for the management of the university system's energy, water, and waste bills. Their decision making process was historically a top-down endeavor for the institution's near hundred-year history. There was a general perception by the students, faculty, staff and administrators occupying the buildings, many of them for decades, that the Facilities department was an uncompassionate monolith, with no interest or concern for the needs of those in the academic community who actually used the buildings.

Presenting at national conferences with hundreds of campuses represented, I have asked audience members to raise their hand if they agree with this perception. Since most hands go up, I suspect that while rarely documented, this view of Facilities is commonplace at many campuses across the nation. This bottom-up, top-down tension seemed to be at the crux of the deadlock suffocating the opportunity for change at campuses across the country. Faculty and staff felt working with Facilities managers was hopeless and as such accepted that there was little chance of change. In addition to path dependency, risk aversion, and the complexity and uncertainty of the wicked challenge of comprehensive systemic change, I was challenged to understand this top-down tension so that it could be liberated allowing change to occur. But where to begin? Armed with all that I had learned from academia, I put the books away and started knocking on doors to see what I could learn from the stakeholders in this hundred-year-old campus stalemate.

PART 2

30 Axioms for Surfing Change

CHAPTER 4

Bridging for Change

I already knew from discussions with academics at UH that building occupants felt the Facilities department was unresponsive, negligent, and ultimately incapable. Since the Facilities department is largely comprised of engineers, I decided to approach them engineer-to-engineer to learn their intentions first hand.

My initial contact with the facilities engineers at the system's flagship campus, UH Manoa (UHM), immediately revealed another side to the story. My first surprise occurred when they not only were willing to meet with me even though I simply presented myself as a potential student, but enthusiastically offered to provide a tour of a typical mechanical room. Though I held no power or influence, they were eager to connect. During our walk-through I became increasingly surprised and inspired by the other side of the story that never made it to the ears of academia. The engineers began by proudly sharing their energy saving efforts, including a recently installed high-efficiency air conditioning chiller. As I asked about other proven strategies such as occupancy sensors that would turn off the lights in empty rooms or timed air-conditioning shutdowns, I quickly came to understand their perspective. They were well aware of such strategies, and had carefully considered and attempted most of them with little success due to pushback from the academic community.

They described their effort to turn off the air conditioning during the weekend, which would save millions if implemented campus-wide. A prestigious professor had happened by the office that Saturday and called in to the head of facilities to complain. The frustrated engineers had been forced to turn on the entire air conditioning system for the building to cool the one room in use. The engineers shared decades of such attempts to implement energy saving solutions, including clustering computer centers, consolidating class schedules to minimize building use, and designating certain regions of the library for sensitive materials rather than requiring highly accurate controls for the entire building. All had been kyboshed by professors' preferences, which they had sometimes justified by mentioning that they had brought in millions in research funding.

The engineers shared numerous challenging stories such as installing a highly expensive and energy intensive lab, only to rip it out the next year as a professor gained tenure and desired the space to be transformed into a corner office with a view. It was easy to see how they might view the academic world as comprised of obtuse, self-serving individuals who cared more about flexing their power and prestige than considering the bigger picture or common good.

My initial exploration of the administrative landscape at UHM revealed that there was a serious disconnect between top-down efforts by the Facilities department and the bottom-up needs of the community. Yet if they could truly hear each other's perspective as I had, I believed this tension would dissipate. This revealed the opportunity for a solution. By identifying this barrier, it became clear that this tension needed to be replaced with a bridge for things to move forward. From this realization the first two axioms that would drive our efforts took form:

Axiom 1: Every challenge can be turned into an opportunity.

Axiom 2: Replace tensions with bridges.

As I explored every conflict I could think of, from personal spats to wars, all revealed that the stakeholders had become polarized and felt completely justified in their stance with little to no understanding of opposing view points. And through this 'us versus them' polarization, each side had dehumanized the other party. I concluded that this dehumanization is the basis for much conflict and friction. When you can't see another group as human, why treat them with fairness and consideration? To address conflict, the polarization had to be identified and somehow diffused. Through communication with both parties I came to understand that each had indeed dehumanized the other, and believed they were valid in doing so given their experiences. Both sides had taken the actions of the others very personally, even though each was acting from their own perspective to meet their own needs without true ill intent toward the other. The challenge became quite clear: common ground had to be found between the Facilities department and the academic community that would evoke the 'humanness' in each and diffuse the polarization creating Axiom 3:

Axiom 3: Remember those who oppose you are human too.

Only when this truth is recognized can the necessary collaboration take place to implement change.

The more I thought about it, the more I realized that it is entirely possible for people from diametrically opposed philosophical positions to work together on a project they both like for different reasons. For example, companies in Israel and Palestine have come together to install wind turbines on the West

Bank (Kloosterman, 2010). Common ground is not about compromising what you believe in or your values. It's about meeting where the polarized parties already share the same viewpoint and interest. Since the groups still hold diametrically different beliefs, it is not about converting the other, but working together on the common interest, with the collaboration probably lasting as long as the project does. Such coalitions can be temporary, shifting, and constantly working — to create change you must be willing to always be IN change. This is best described by the following axiom:

Axiom 4: Coalitions do not mean compromising values.

Often polarized parties believe the only way to move out of a stalemate is to sacrifice or compromise their values. They are at a standstill because they are not willing to do anything as they feel they will lose what they believe in. Yet each party can hold onto what they believe in, agree to disagree on their core values, and instead focus on what they already agree on, forming Axiom 5:

Axiom 5: Coalitions collaborate on common ground.

I experienced this in a situation close to home, which forced me to implement these foundational axioms in my own life.

It began when I moved into a new apartment. It felt like a big move for me since I had been happily living with my brother for nearly three years and my reason for relocating was because he was moving back to the mainland. I knew I had to turn the challenge of living on my own again without family in the middle of the Pacific into an opportunity. I managed to do so by finding an amazing new apartment right on the ocean with my favorite surf break as my front yard. Rather than feel sad at the loss of sharing a home with my best friend and close family member, I began looking forward to the excitement of enjoying the ocean breeze and sunsets with friends in my own space. I was ready to embrace all the joys of living alone again. On my first day, I savored unpacking my things to make my new home my own.

I had moved within the same building from a smaller unit further from the ocean. My friends and neighbors dropped by all day to congratulate me on my upgrade, and to make sure I wasn't too sad missing my brother. I felt understood, supported and ultimately happy until my favorite time of day came — sunset.

As I walked toward my front doors just a few feet from the ocean wall ready to enjoy the view, I was overcome with something that would prove to plague my every evening — cigarette smoke. And not just random smoke, but smoke from friends and neighbors who knew I just moved in, and chose to sit in front of my door on the ocean wall and smoke anyway. It was a very rare reaction for me, but I felt incredibly hurt, disappointed and violated. They must have forgotten I moved in? I looked at them and we smiled at each other as usual. Then I said, "You probably don't realize it but smoke is drifting in. Don't worry about it tonight, but I just wanted to let you know so we can figure it out!" Their faces fell and with those few words, somehow a war was started.

I came to realize the impact of that interaction a couple days later when I had a friend over for dinner. As we settled with our Thai take-out on my lanai, we were soon engulfed in cigarette smoke. Thinking simple communication is all that would be needed, I leaned over the wall to let them know that I had a guest with me who was allergic to smoke and asked if they would mind moving for a bit. They responded that they would prefer to stay where they were.

I was completely shocked, and tried to clarify, "But I have a student here who is allergic to smoke and you're comfortable with asking us to move, yet you won't?"

I was met with angry words "We're not moving! You know we smoke here and have for years!"

I was blown away that I had to state something that seemed to be the obvious, "But no one lived here! Now that I do, shouldn't things change?"

"We're not moving," were their final words, and I was left speechless.

I began to research my options and found out the building management had no grounds for action since the ocean wall was public property. And while I had no legal ground, a cancer hotline said they could send me "no-smoking" signs to post and I excitedly ordered them. But something felt wrong. Posting those signs would just increase the polarization since I was treating them as criminals and violators. Both sides had fallen into pre-scripted stereotypes that allowed us to replace our personal connection with something less personal. I had labeled them as insensitive smokers and they labeled me as a self-righteous non-smoker. I had stopped seeing them as human and they had certainly stopped seeing me as human. It was a stand-off and I knew I had to use our own theories to diffuse the situation. Despite my outrage I had to see them as human. To begin this process I completely put the smoking situation aside and started treating them as human. I decided to be the friend to them I had been for years before my move.

I began by offering them some extra frozen strawberries I needed to get rid of to make room in my freezer. It was a sincere gesture and they must have felt my warmth because, despite their surprised silence, they put their hands out and accepted them. I continued to happily and sincerely say hi when we passed and struck up conversations as we had for years about recipes, gardening, and surf gear. After a few weeks I truly remembered how lovely they were and enjoyed our spontaneous friendly interactions. The polarization had been diffused and we again saw each other as human. It was natural one day to discuss the issue of smoking as two friends facing a problem, rather than two opposing forces.

I sincerely listened as I would to any friend and was finally able to see their side. Sunset was the one time of day they connected as a family after a long day's work and the ocean wall was their location of choice since they could watch their daughter swimming and playing. They had been yelled at and treated poorly due to their smoking for years, so they already felt defensive when it came to complaining non-smokers. They had attempted to be considerate by trying many locations along the wall in the past and found their smoke bothered groups of people no matter where they sat. They felt they had nowhere else to go. When I moved in they began burning incense thinking it would mask the smoke.

They had put a lot more consideration into it than I had thought, and they had been making an effort. So when I asked them to move it seemed to them that their efforts were completely not appreciated and that I was acting with a sense of entitlement and judgment, demanding that they give up their daily family connection. I was surprised to learn that from their perspective, they had felt equally outraged and violated. Our core values remained opposites — I would never understand feeling the right to smoke while they would never understand being told not to smoke. Yet we no longer took it personally. And we had found common ground we already agreed on — we wanted peace on the home front.

I explained that it had never been my intent to be rude and that I hadn't understood what that time meant to them. I also said it wasn't fair that they had lumped me in with others in the past who had treated them poorly. They agreed. And when I explained that I had experienced them as insensitive to the challenge of moving somewhere new, especially without my brother, they understood as well. We each realized we had seen the other as completely insensitive and thus inhuman, hence the stand-off. While we didn't agree, we finally understood each other.

Since we saw each other as human, it was natural to want the other to be happy. I sincerely wanted them to enjoy their time together as a family, and they wanted me to enjoy my new home. So we decided to share the space. They would move to the beach, which was away from all the buildings during low tide that occurred often during the fall and winter. In the meantime, I would let them know during the summer what days I needed a smoke-free sunset and they would find somewhere away from the ocean. While we had originally wanted the space to ourselves, we still found the common ground of wanting to be friendly neighbors and crafted a creative solution without changing our opposing core beliefs.

Could the same diffusion of such a gross polarization occur on campus? It would require a great amount of non-judgment listening and engagement of all stakeholders. Unlike my neighbors and I who shared the same small space so our paths crossed continually, academics and Facilities engineers were rarely in the same place at once. There was a tangible focal point of interest for both of us — the ocean wall right outside my door. What would cause academia and Facilities to communicate? They needed some sort of common ground that provided a tangible opportunity to connect, face their opposition and hopefully eventually collaborate.

The opportunity to create such a common ground presented itself when I was asked to be the student coordinator of an initiative called Sustainable Saunders. Saunders Hall is a typical building within the University of Hawaii ten-campus system. Built in 1974, each of its seven stories houses a different department within the College of Social Sciences. In 2006 the Dean of Social Sciences, the Legislatures in Residence, the Public Policy Center, and the Office of Sustainability designated Saunders Hall as the campus pilot project where new technologies and change-making projects could be trialed. Those that proved successful could be rolled out throughout the campus and beyond.

While it wasn't obvious to new students, a lot of groundwork had been laid on campus and this initiative was just one example. In fact, so many stakeholders had been talking about the need for change that the idea had been brewing for years. They realized a common ground was needed and I felt honored to be asked to help coordinate. We all hoped Sustainable Saunders would provide the unprecedented opportunity to bridge the many previously isolated departments, and also to address the long-standing conflict between academia and Facilities.

Again, we realized how much groundwork was already in progress when the UHM Chancellor's Office announced an Energy Summit on October 24, 2006, just following the creation of Sustainable Saunders. The campus leader at that time, Denise Konan, was a much-loved faculty member who had stepped into the challenging position of Interim Chancellor. An Economist at heart, she was awakened to the great drain on the campus's energy bill when she was invited to sit at the head table at the Christmas dinner of Hawaii's main utility, the Hawaiian Electric Company (HECO). When she realized it was because UHM paid one of the highest energy bills in the state she was inspired to launch change. She demonstrated stakeholder engagement by bringing all the players together, including academia, Facilities, the utilities, renewable energy companies, and mainland consultants, to explore how to address our whopping energy bill. The result was UHM's first Clean Energy Policy with the following goals:

- 30% reduction in campus energy use by 2012

- 50% reduction in campus energy use by 2015

- 25% of campus energy supplied by renewable sources by 2020

- Energy and water self-sufficiency for the campus by 2050

Previous to the announcement of this policy, the various departments I had tried to engage in taking action had not been able to justify allotting time or resources no matter how great their interest was. After the summit, doors that had been closed flew open. I was repeatedly asked, "Is this in line with the Chancellor's goals?" When I was able to answer that it was, I found that even those who did not have an interest or passion in change could be engaged in supporting our efforts. While I had wanted to believe that progress could be made without the prioritization from top-level leadership, I could not deny that clear direction from above had been paramount in engaging support and I became convinced of the following:

Axiom 6: Change starts with clear direction from top-level leadership.

To launch systemic change, clear prioritization, direction, and measurable goals must come from top-level leadership.

At the Energy Summit the Chancellor announced that the intent of the Sustainable Saunders initiative was to empower community action as a new hope for achieving UHM's Clean Energy Policy goals. I wondered what the literature said about this approach and found that grassroots efforts that are not well linked to the institutionalized procedures and processes often result in groups failing to implement their goals (Innes, 1992, p. 451). I concluded that systemic change would be much more successful in implementation if action from the community level was linked to top-level priorities. This led to the following axiom:

Axiom 7: Grassroots change is more likely to succeed if it is in line with top-level priorities.

This is not to say that grassroots change must be created in response to top-level priorities, but rather that it will be more successful when they align. It should also be noted that it is not far fetched to think that grassroots level and top-level priorities would be in alignment. Leaders rarely create visions from nowhere; they usually respond to a larger flow of ideas that grassroots groups are also privy to. In the case of the Chancellor, she was responding to economic realities and global issues that many students and faculty also felt concerned about. Her creation of top-level priorities and grassroots interest to launch Sustainable Saunders were both in response to the same information, hence a natural alignment.

Sustainable Saunders was all the more possible since the goals of the initiative were in line with the goals of the campus community, and the Chancellor's leadership rallied support, engaging previously polarized stakeholders. Yet I was the only one hired as a graduate student assistant for the project and I was given no funding. Despite lots of hype and high expectations, I had no money and no power, except for alignment with top-level goals. I set out with the hypothesis that change could occur if one had enough passion and could interconnect and leverage the community. I knew it was time to assemble a team.

CHAPTER 5

Change Agents Unite

Without the capability to pay anyone, the only option was to assemble a team of volunteers. If we were to be successful, the team would need to be skilled, passionate, and able to create an incredible group synergy beyond the mere sum of its parts. Yet I was told that UHM had one of the most apathetic student bodies in the US where students were much more interested in escaping campus to surf than in getting involved. Yet the 'surfing' students I met did not seem apathetic to me. They were adventurous, stoked on life, enjoyed challenges, felt connected to their social and natural surroundings and truly cared for Hawaii. I posted signs around campus to advertise an open invitation for anyone to attend a focus group if they wanted to be part of real change for the betterment of Hawaii. Despite warnings of probable disinterest, over fifty people showed up.

Next I selected a steering committee of eight students based on their authentic passion and their demonstrated ability to get involved and take positive action. For example Sean Connelly, a creative architecture student, had installed large displays around campus that had silent but flashing warning sirens that drew pedestrians closer to investigate. Once you reached the large wooden sandwich board attached to the siren, there were two small words that said everything, 'Save Hawaii.'

Another student, Tamara Armstrong, handed me her business card for 'Kailua Recycling,' the operation she ran with her friends to provide services to a community lacking curbside pick up. As she explained her business model of profiting from collecting the recycling as well as the ample tips from her pleased clientele, I couldn't help asking why she didn't just surf on Saturdays. Her answer said it all: "I love growing a business that does good for Hawaii!" These students were not only thrilled to be invited to apply their passion and creativity on campus; they were inspired to find kindred spirits. They immediately became friends, surfing buddies, and committed teammates based on their common passion for change and proven ability to take positive action. These students didn't just have the theory; they demonstrated their ability to implement. The amazing dynamic that emerged when these students came together inspired the following axiom:

Axiom 8: Passion + Positive Action = Effective Change Agent

While there were no personal conflicts on the first semester's team, we needed to plan for many future years and cohorts of students, where conflict might arise. Diversities might clash, or a team member might offend someone, drop the ball or generally jar the flow of projects. To ensure the team culture would live on, even if the students changed every semester, we work-shopped what made the experience special and formed the list of core values found at the beginning of this book. When things got murky or out of sorts, we looked to the Core Values (see p. xi) to keep us on track and sort through situations. For example, one semester a team member preferring a vegan diet very much wanted all our events to be vegan and it was starting to become a conflict amongst team members who felt judged for eating free-range meat. Food is a very personal subject and it was the one time in four years where tension ran high on the team.

We were able to look to our value of "perspectives, not agendas" that clearly stated our value of promoting many options that worked toward sustainable practices. In the area of food, some consider local, free-range meat a sustainable choice and we did not see it our organization's responsibility to promote one path. Also, there were many organizations that already did this. We wanted to provide many options so that participants at our events could be exposed to choices and decide for themselves. The core values allowed us to keep passion and positive action alive by diffusing conflict.

In the spirit of diversity, another key to the success of our group was that we were an interdisciplinary team. Since the problems we wanted to address were beyond the scope of any one discipline, many perspectives were needed to answer complex questions and address broad issues characterized by 'wicked' problems (Klein, 1990, p. 11). Indeed the original members of the 2006-2007 Sustainable Saunders steering committee below

represented architecture, engineering, tourism management, indigenous medicine, environmental studies, and microbiology.

Our team was evenly divided by gender and half were graduate students while the other half was undergraduates. A few had been born and raised in Hawaii, while others came from Canada, California, New Mexico, and Colorado. We hoped this diversity would foster unique synergy and collaborations that could achieve transformative results. There was immediate chemistry in the group and creative ideas flowed as students sparked off each other's unique perspective and knowledge. Our theory held true: In addition to being passionate and driven for positive action, members of an effective team of change agents must be diverse and interdisciplinary.

Axiom 9: Diversity + Interdisciplinary = Creative Solutions

From the beginning, we committed to meeting for one hour every week and treating that meeting seriously, with members calling ahead of time if they were going to be absent. In this way 'flaking out' was eliminated and all eight members were present at every meeting for the entire first semester, which strengthened the group synergy. But it was going to take more that just commitment to keep the momentum — the entire process had to be engaging.

In addition to ensuring that the students had what the team needed to be successful, we strove to ensure that the team dynamic offered what the students needed to stay inspired and engaged. I had participated in many community action groups that lost members over time due to frustrating and ineffective processes and I was determined to ensure this wouldn't happen. We needed to foster a unique culture of engagement.

Gradually it became clear from student feedback that the group's culture of meaningful interaction and optimal experience prompted them to remain engaged and inspired for years. Even students who graduated made arrangements with their employers to attend our meetings for their love of the experience. Four years after the formation of the team, alumni who now have careers as change agents but still consider themselves team members and enjoy staying engaged, manage our web site, Face Book, Twitter, Google Calendar, and Google Group. This is because the team dynamic had consistently fostered optimal experience for the students, creating the following axiom:

Axiom 10: Optimal Experience = Effective Change Agent

One of my students gave me the book, *Flow, The Psychology of Optimal Experience*, by Mihaly Csikszentmihalyi, because I had shared my vision of teaching a course called 'Flowgenomics' that I hoped would describe our team dynamic. Written by a professor and psychologist, this book provided a theoretical basis for Axiom 10 by summarizing decades of research on the positive aspects of human experience, including joy, creativity, and the process of total involvement with life, which the author called flow (Csikszentmihalyi, 1990, p. xi). A flow activity was defined as providing a sense of discovery, a creative feeling of propelling the person into a new reality while transforming the self through growth (Csikszentmihalyi, 1990, p. 74). For an activity to create flow, it must have rules that require the learning of skills, set up goals, provide feedback and make control possible (Csikszentmihalyi, 1990, p. 72).

When activities have these attributes and are in line with someone's natural curiosity and interest, people can become completely absorbed and ultimately have an enjoyable, optimal experience. This type of activity was central to our team since students took on projects of a manageable scope, created measurable goals and were able to take measurements, do research, write reports and have autonomy over their contributions.

Figure 1 shows how skill and challenge level create flow.

When both skill and challenge levels are high, students are having an optimal experience. But flow is a moving target. As students repeatedly engage in an activity, it gets easier for them and becomes less challenging as their skill levels increase. Therefore,

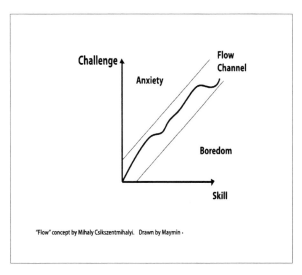

"Flow" concept by Mihaly Csikszentmihalyi. Drawn by Maymin ·

Figure 1: Human Experience of Various Skill and Challenge Levels (Csikszentmihalyi, 1990, p. 74).

more challenging projects must be continually created so the enjoyable experience of flow can continue (Csikszentmihalyi, 1990, p. 75). I found this repeatedly with the team. We would master a skill, become bored and come to meetings looking for a new level of challenge to stretch our abilities. It became obvious that change agents will maximize our capabilities when our challenges and skills are ever-increasing and grow in proportion to each other. This is because change agents will rise to new challenges when we are enjoying an optimal experience. Thus:

Axiom 11: Keep raising the bar to continually create optimal experiences.

These theories from Csikszentmihalyi supported much of what I had learned from my rather unique upbringing. To say that a women opening an unheard of business in a small town in Canada in the early 1970s was a rarity would be an understatement. Yet that's just what my mother did. She converted the first floor of our house to a Montessori school, a form of education that was nearly non-existent in our country, let alone in my hometown of St. Thomas, Ontario, with a population of 30,000. Yet she made it a huge success and I spent many after-school hours there for years. I loved seeing how students grew through their own self-directed engagement, and they apparently did too. To this day when I run into her fully-grown students decades later they still say how their memories at our school are some of their favorites. The following summarizes how the Montessori method of education views optimal experience for learning, growing, and contributing:

> Dr. Maria Montessori, Italy's first female physician, believed that no human being is educated by another person. She instead believed that one must train themselves, and a truly educated individual continues learning beyond the classroom because they are motivated from within by a natural curiosity and love for knowledge. Dr. Montessori felt that the goal of education should not be to fill a person with facts, but rather to cultivate his or her own natural desire to learn. In the Montessori classroom this objective is approached in two ways: first, by allowing each person to experience the excitement of learning by his or her own choice rather than by being forced; and second, by helping to perfect one's natural tools for learning, so that abilities will be at a maximum in future learning situations (Montessori, 1912, p. 1).

Our team was designed to incorporate Csikszentmihaly's flow and Montessori's self-directed learning, to optimizing each individual's experience, thus creating an effective team. Students became change agents by being supported in cultivating their natural desire to learn and engage in tasks. We came to call this a 'pull' not 'push' philosophy. We encouraged each other to tap into what really pulled us, and to not sign up for something if we felt pushed. It was difficult at first to tell the difference, but we came up with some useful rules of thumb. If we were using the word 'should' it probably was a push or something you thought you had to do, but didn't really want to. We reminded each other not to 'should' on yourself. The diversity of the team was key since nearly every task was accomplished through someone's pull. Due to the diversity of the group, I reminded the team that if they signed up for something they didn't really want to do, they were taking the opportunity away from a teammate who actually really wanted to do it. As surprising as it may seem, in four years every task has been accomplished through someone's pull.

Axiom 12: Pull not Push = Team Stamina

Whether they had the relevant skills or experience to accomplish the task they were pulled to didn't matter as long as they held a sincere interest. They were encouraged to engage their team members and to seek mentorship from others and myself, but they were ultimately each responsible for self-directed learning. In Hawaiian this personal self-responsibility is called your *kuleana*. It is often described as your duty or responsibility, but I believe it means something deeper. Not being Hawaiian, I can only describe what that word has come to mean to me. I feel my *kuleana* is my purpose aligned with truly knowing myself and cultivating what I have to offer the world. *Kuleana* to me is honoring this purpose with integrity and accountability, and encompasses everything from doing my best in school to being there for students when they need me to writing this book.

Whenever a student committed to a task from a sincere pull, it became part of their *kuleana* and they were to see it through. They agreed to communicate with the team honestly if a task became too overwhelming or stressful, so we could help them get back into flow by supporting them in finding the resources they needed. Sometimes it became apparent that the task really wasn't part of their *kuleana* so another teammate gave it a shot. Stress was not to be a natural part of what we did. Any student feeling stressed, afraid or overwhelmed was to take this as a sign to reach out to get back into flow.

Another way of identifying a task as a pull is that after engaging in it you have more energy than when you began. Like having lunch with a good friend, you should feel sparked up after your time with a task. If you felt drained, it could be a push and you should reevaluate. Another possibility of the energy drain was a perfectionist approach, which we called the 'perfectionism vortex.' Since we were so committed to doing a great job, students would sometimes feel overwhelmed with all the possibilities while lacking direction. We combated this syndrome by ensuring all projects were done in groups, even if it was just two students. They would keep each other on track, providing support and avoiding spinning out — plus it was more fun. While it was a simple concept, the following axiom proved one of our most useful:

Axiom 13: Working together keeps things on track.

Another way of combating the 'perfectionism vortex' came from brainstorming roadblocks, maintaining direction as a group, and using our meetings as a think tank. As our main point of contact was a weekly meeting, this had to be made exciting somehow. While most view meetings as a necessary evil, I thought they should be the highlight of the week to keep everyone including me engaged and productive. With such great group synergy, we never needed an agenda and rather ran meetings according to who was 'bursting' the most with what they wanted to contribute.

In steering the meetings, a problem would be framed and everyone would share his or her 'burst,' as I watched the clock and steered us toward conclusion. Rather than tightly control our time together, I allowed the dialogue to flow, only interrupting to keep the bursts focused on solutions to the currently posed problem. I also interrupted if someone attempted to dominate since one of our core values is that intentions are valued over agendas. In this way we did not allow one voice to promote an agenda or perspective, but honored many different viewpoints to be brought forward with the intention of collaborating, not dominating. While many who chair meetings hesitate to interrupt, this actually becomes a welcome role of the leader when the team knows the intent is to make the most use of everyone's time in accomplishing the goals all members care about. This also achieved another goal that everyone agreed upon and appreciated: our meetings almost always ended exactly on time.

The dynamic nature of our collaboration fostered such creative synergy that we quickly formed solutions that were so clear and exciting that we reached consensus on our path forward for every challenge, no matter how complex. Thus we ensured meetings were a 'no drone zone' and viewed them as follows:

Axiom 14: Meetings are for creative, collaborative problem solving.

Rather than bringing a list of accomplishments to our meetings, we brought a list of challenges. Instead of giving reports to prove that we had progressed on our projects, we used our time together to engage everyone in creative problem solving. 'Work-shopping' with so many diverse minds was such a novelty to all of us that, as I had hoped, many students said our meeting was the highlight of their week due to the optimal experience they enjoyed.

Our team dynamic came together quickly and within the first semester we had most of these axioms in place. We wanted to give our team a name besides "Student Steering Committee," which felt pretty dry given our unique, dynamic culture. To ensure that the community knew we were collaborators and valued their support, we named our team HUB, which stands for Help Us Bridge. This may be the single most important marketing strategy that set our organization apart. It established that we knew we needed help and support and had no intention of working outside or around the system. This also differentiated us from the 'watch us protest' students of yesteryear. We wanted to be known for being of service and writing excellent proposals, not for making angry demands.

The name HUB also reflects our two-fold mission: to implement change-making projects at Saunders Hall and to interconnect as many individuals and organizations as possible for change. We created a motto of **live, connect, create** to represent our goals of living our principles, connecting the campus and extended community, and creating unique solutions. An ancient symbol for energy became our logo when we changed the colors to a blue ring around a green circle. Some people see the Earth surrounded by the sky; some see an island in the ocean. We see blue-sky envisioning that is grounded in proven green principles.

Called 'the Dot,' the simplicity of the logo had another purpose. We envisioned that one day the University of Hawaii would be the world's accreditation center for all products and services that demonstrated best practices in terms of environmental and social responsibility. UH could draw on our many academic experts and researchers to create criteria for every type of product or service sold. For example, perhaps clothing would have to be made from renewable sources such as bamboo and organic cotton, as was the case for all our t-shirts, and would have to be printed with non-toxic soy based ink and sewn by workers being paid fair wages. If a pair of shorts from a company such as Nike met the criteria, they could incorporate the Dot with their logo, perhaps placing their well known 'swoosh' inside the circle. In this way consumers everywhere could quickly and easily identify products and service providers that met standardized, well-researched criteria. This seemed all the more possible since the Dot was a symbol everyone responded to. Students made it into art, buttons, painted it on t-shirts and pencil cases, and used it in graffiti. It had a viral effect and soon the Dot was everywhere on campus.

Together, our name, logo (shown with dot as an apple), motto and mission gave us an identity that unified us and helped people get to know us quickly. We wanted to work with the administration AND academia, honor path dependency AND create transformative change. We saw Sustainable Saunders as the common ground that could allow all this to take place and felt it was our *kuleana* to maximize its potential. As we sat down at our early meetings we faced our first complex and overwhelming challenge: How would we engage all the stakeholders to maximize Saunders' potential to catalyze change?

CHAPTER 6

Interactively
Launching Change

In contemplating the question of how to engage stakeholders, we were looking for more than buy-in; we were looking to interconnect everyone for ideas, support, guidance, and innovation. So often planning is thought of as a list of tasks with owners and due dates, but the form relationships take with stakeholders is often of greater benefit than the tasks themselves. We had our next challenge: How could we create an event that kicked off the Sustainable Saunders initiative in a way that shared our vision but still left plenty of room for input, and that would engage everyone to contribute and believe their efforts would be valued?

While we had no funding, we wanted a thousand people to attend and we wanted all of Hawaii to be excited about Sustainable Saunders by the end of the semester. We decided that our first step would be to approach the Hawaiian Electrical Company (HCEO) to ask for sponsorship of the event. Our budget was $12,000 to promote and to hold an all day networking event followed by a concert so that the initiative would not only be perceived as educational, but also a party. HECO showed their enthusiasm and support by offering to match up to half the budget.

Their response inspired us to collaborate and build a network even before the party had begun. We got to work and applied for student event grants, private sponsorships from companies such as Inter Island Solar, Hawaii's oldest solar company, and many channels of media sponsors, especially those with large existing email lists such as the Hawaii Health Guide. We came back to HECO a month later with $6,000 raised in monetary and in-kind donations.

Impressed with our commitment and true to their word, HECO presented a check for our Launch Party to the tune of $6,000 in a ceremony with all the campus upper administration, and a hundred staff and faculty. The movement had begun.

Through much collaboration, the Sustainable Saunders Interactive Launch Party was created. Held on Earth Day, April 22, 2007, the seven floors of Saunders Hall were divided into fifteen theme areas including recycling and composting (see photo below), bicycling, climate change, energy and water conservation, renewable energy, architectural design, sustainability education, food security and organic agriculture. Each area had free food samples offered by local restaurants and vendors, and various musicians played in the open central courtyard, creating an interactive party atmosphere on all floors.

Over one hundred experts including professors, politicians, students, business leaders, non-profit organizations and community leaders received special invitations to be present in their theme area to speak informally with the community about their topic. Honoring these experts served to provide information that enhanced the discussions that day and also engaged many leaders throughout the state from the very beginning of the process. Each theme area was hung with white paper covering the walls so that the hundreds of students, faculty, staff, experts, and community members could jot down their own ideas graffiti-style for evolving Saunders Hall. The intent was that the HUB would then attempt to implement these suggestions in conjunction with all the stakeholders.

Given that over a hundred invited experts and a thousand community members attended and filled the graffiti paper, and that the HUB was featured on most newspapers and television station in Hawaii, the event was deemed a success. Our efforts became a public service announcement that played for months on local television and by the end of the semester we were known throughout Hawaii just as we had hoped. Much more valuable than the recognition was the momentum that was building, as so many now felt part of what had been launched on Earth Day. Before we did anything, we had very publicly asked the community what they wanted, and had provided a unique forum for sharing and creating a common vision. And by honoring those already working on these challenges and by inviting them as experts to guide the process, we ensured that what emerged was integrated with what already existed, honoring path dependency.

We collected hundreds of email addresses that day, and at every event for the next four years. We built a free on-line Google group where members could post opportunities and events related to sustainability in Hawaii. Following the launch event we continued the integration by asking various experts to share their expertise and current efforts at a weekly energy education series that was attended by the HUB's Energy Team and was open to the community through an invitation to our Google group. Here we learned about lighting, air conditioning, energy audits, plug loads and more. Every presentation was followed by a passionate discussion on how we could apply the expert's ideas to Saunders Hall. For example, a HECO engineer pointed out locations of inefficient incandescent lighting that we would never have thought to look for such as in staircases. By changing 113 of these bulbs to efficient CFLs (compact fluorescent lights) Saunders saved over $6000 every year. And HECO picked up the bill for the CFLs with their rebate program. The key to our early widespread impact was that as a new organization attempting to make change, we had honored path dependency by integrating with and building on existing efforts, forming the following axiom:

Axiom 15: Change must build on existing efforts.

CHAPTER 7

Growing Change

Student groups over the last many decades have earned a reputation for not honoring path dependency. Since they graduate and move on, their efforts are viewed as 'flash-in-the-pan' organizations that are transient on campus and cannot understand issues that have existed long before them and will exist long after they graduate. Yet the very goal of being a student is to quickly grasp issues and develop solutions. Students naturally excel in these skills. And many students move on to do even bigger and better things, just not within the context of the campus. Their continued transience is a positive, natural function of the campus. And fresh ideas and energy ever rotating into a group should be an asset. So it's not their inability to get up to speed that render campus groups ineffective. I propose it is the short time frame in which students want action to occur that creates friction that stifles change.

Many student groups seem like they act from a sense of entitlement since they want quick results due to their short time horizon on campus. The demand for quick action hasn't matched the path dependency of bureaucratic processes and the cultural norms of those who have been working within them for decades. The inability to recognize this friction in time frames has been the fatal flaw of many campus groups striving for change.

Policy theorists have actually categorized different types of change processes as shown in Figure 2 below (Kelly, Cashore, Bernstein, & Auld, 2009, p. 15). The typical aggressive policy change advocated by students can be described as fast and cumulative, such as the 'classic paradigmatic' approach. While this type of intense change may seem desirable, it may actually close off path dependent policy pathways with, possibly, the most transformative potential. An alternative option that reflects the HUB approach is 'progressive incremental policies,' which has a better opportunity for acceptance (Kelly, Cashore, Bernstein, & Auld, 2009, p. 15).

	Tempo Or Speed Of Change	
Directionality	Fast	Slow
Cumalative	Classic paradigmatic 	Progressive Incremental 
In Equilibrium	Faux paradigmatic 	Classic Incremental 

Figure 2: Taxonomy of Change and Stability (Kelly, Cashore, Bernstein, & Auld, 2009, p. 14)

We found that collaborating to introduce 'progressive increments' in the form of slow, cumulative changes best honors path dependency, and addresses risk aversions, leading to the following axiom:

Axiom 16: Slow, cumulative changes make consistent progress.

While each increment is small enough to be accepted and implemented, the key is selecting increments that contribute to a cumulative total that brings us closer to the preferred future (Kelly, Cashore, Bernstein, & Auld, 2009, p. 14). *Progressive Incremental* differs from the classic perception of *incremental* since the overall path continually moves toward overarching goals. This means that each increment, no matter how small, is of value if it moves *irreversibly* toward the end goal. If there is pushback from the community or if they are so unhappy with the activity that they undo it, then nothing was accomplished. I like to think of this in terms of a simple equation I learned for work in engineering. The equation is:

$$W = F \times d \text{ (Work = Force times distance)}$$

For measurable work to occur, there has to be force on something, but that something also has to move. If you push on a brick wall you may feel like you're doing a lot of work, but since the wall does not move, no work is done. If distance equals zero, work equals zero. I have sat through many meetings where people are, as I say, 'talking about talking about it.' There are a lot of ideas and perhaps even great amounts of effort, yet nothing really gets done. This force without movement does not equal real work. Simply stated, projects implemented must stay implemented for effort to contribute toward change. For example, in addition to simply being considerate, valuing the experience of the community when implementing a pilot or project is a highly necessary function for success. For the progression to continue, the increment must also be irreversible. If it isn't undone, progress occurs and eventually over time the overarching goals are accomplished. This formed the following axiom:

Axiom 17: Each increment must move irreversibly toward the end goal.

The Sustainable Saunders initiative further honored path dependency by incorporating 'chance elements' as valued increments. Such events are called 'wild cards' in Futures Studies. Our open-door policy has thankfully resulted in many students showing up mid-semester over the years wanting to do something completely out of left field from our current efforts like create an art installation out of recycled glass, shoot a video of our projects, or grow food on campus. Many organizations I've participated in often turn them away saying this is beyond our scope at the moment. We decided to do the opposite. If someone comes with a burst, as long as they are not misaligned with our overarching goal, our immediate reaction is to support their efforts, even if we don't understand how they will fit into the bigger picture.

Repeatedly we have been shown that such projects don't remain outliers for long. An art contest will emerge down the road for recycled materials and with our glass sculpture already created, we gain the edge with the first entry submitted. The video of our projects was exactly what we needed to accompany a grant proposal a few months after it was completed. And students that were working on the idea of growing food had a plan ready to go when our much loved head of Social Sciences, Dean Dubanoski, announced a food kiosk going in at Saunders Hall. We have found incorporating wild cards to be one of the most interesting, fun, and surprisingly useful parts of our process creating the following axiom:

Axiom 18: Incorporate 'wild cards' in line with your overarching goals.

Incorporating wild cards also has unexpected beneficial ripple effects even after implementation. For example, the Dean had been envisioning a gathering place for the many departments, which were each contained on a separate floor of the building and had little opportunity to interconnect and collaborate. The HUB viewed this as an opportunity to integrate with the community since the idea already had acceptance, an internal champion, and momentum.

After consulting with Facilities, urban planning students, the campus's landscape architect and many others, the obvious choice for the new seating area was recycled plastic lumber picnic tables that would last twenty years since they are mildew and termite resistent and cannot be carved for graffitti. This collaborative brainstorming session served an unexpected purpose in that all the participants felt ownership and stepped up to help.

When one of our earliest and continual supportors, Roxanne Adams from Grounds and Landscaping, learned we would have to pay nearly $1,700 to import each table, she introduced us to the Marine Science department. Their machine shop operators taught us how to build the tables, and even cut and prepared the pieces to simplify the process.

We soon realized that we too often outsource what people right in our community would be happy to do. In the end they only charged for the materials, which totalled about $3,000 for seven tables, nearly $9,000 less than we would have paid to import. Since Dean Dubanoski had allocated $7,000 for the project he was extremely pleased and asked if there was anything the HUB wanted in return. We asked for the remaining $4,000 to apply to other projects, which he granted, and we were finally able to purchase the equipment we required to perform energy assessments for the building.

While we hadn't expected to achieve our first funding from this effort, we also didn't expect the incredible response we received from the community in the form of emails and comments of appreciation from the building occupants. Some had been in Saunders Hall for forty years and had never had the opportunity to sit nearby outside and chat with a collegue from a different department. When we first placed picnic tables on the open balcony of the seventh floor of Saunders, there was limited impact since these served just the seventh floor community. It was only when we placed seven picnic tables around the building for all to access that the community felt our intention to be of service in making positive change. We realized that for a new change-making organization like ours to be accepted by a community, initial projects must serve the community's identified needs, and must be highly visible and equally accessible to all in the community. This insight is summarized as follows:

Axiom 19: Initial projects must be highly visible and widely accessible.

This was also accomplished by doing a waste audit, often called a 'dumpster dive', on the front lawn of Saunders Hall, showing how we were literally willing to get our hands dirty. We then implemented recycling bins on every floor and through a subsequent dive, found that we had diverted 70% of the bottles from the land fill. We displayed the waste audit findings outside the elevators on the main floor so that all could see the results of our collective efforts. After these two projects, there was no one in Saunders Hall who hadn't encountered one of our efforts to be of service.

CHAPTER 8

Implementing Change

Now that those in the Saunders community who had originally been wary and even resistant to our organization were opening to our efforts, we needed to determine the first step in reducing our energy bill. With my engineering experience as my greatest personal asset, I shared with the team an important axiom from my field:

Axiom 20: You can't manage what you don't measure.

To create measurable goals a baseline must first be established. A baseline is a snapshot of the current metrics of interest. For example, electricity and water bills measure the current use of resources, and waste audits measure the generation of waste. These measures can be benchmarked, which means comparing them against best practices for comparable buildings in comparable conditions to identify realistic goals. Progress is measured over time by continuing to use the same method of measure to track the metrics of interest. In this way evaluating progress becomes a science rather than an estimation.

The Public Policy Center, which originally housed the Sustainable Saunders program, had taken the lead on measurement by installing an electricity meter for the building to establish a baseline of energy use. Now we could measure the impact of each of our projects against this baseline and gauge our success. Once we could measure our progress we had to choose a goal to drive our efforts. Since the campus's goal was to reduce energy use by 30% in five years (from 2007 to 2012), we selected a 30% reduction in the building's energy use in one year without spending a cent to prove that it could be accomplished much more quickly and without additional cost.

This was viewed as incredibly ambitious; I was told repeatedly that we had 'bit off more than we could chew' and that we had been set up to fail. Yet, we looked at the energy use of similar buildings and they were using considerably less energy than Saunders Hall. And by setting a goal that would break the limitations of our perceived capabilities, we created a worthy challenge that would require, and thus hopefully inspire, innovation.

We realized that achieving the goal would be such an accomplishment that it would be so satisfying! And since the result of achieving the goal would be in alignment with the agreed upon preferred future of the campus, it could foster widespread engagement. We believed that for a goal to inspire change, it must result in a scenario beyond business as usual and be in line with the community's preferred future. Simply put, everyone should look at the goal and think, "I want that." This solidified the following axiom for goal setting:

Axiom 21: An overarching goal must inspire change.

As we began to contemplate what projects would be worth our effort in moving toward our goal, we needed criteria for assessment. How would we know if a project actually created a worthy change? Traditionally many organizational decisions from procurement to policy are made from a single bottom line: money. When businesses speak of striving to increase or fatten their bottom line they are simply trying to increase profits. Yet what if every decision also considered whether the people affected, including their culture, health, happiness and fulfillment, where to also benefit? And what if the environment were to also experience a positive result? While the environment, society, and economy were often considered tradeoffs, what if they simultaneously benefited? A framework called the 'triple bottom line' strives to measure the success of initiatives not by economic factors alone, but also by social and environmental benefit. If the decision reduces waste or resource use, improves conditions for society AND increases profits, the triple bottom line of sustainability is satisfied, forming the next axiom:

Axiom 22: Each step must benefit the triple bottom line.

Given this framework, we decided to strive toward change that truly integrates the environment, community, and economy through *synergy*. Simply defined, synergy occurs when the whole is greater than the sum of the individual parts. This word embodies the interconnection of all the various components working together where there is a simultaneous benefit to all. When people the planet and profits simultaneously benefit and are not viewed as trade-offs, the concept of the triple bottom line becomes a very useful rule of thumb to gauge the direction and success of any project or initiative.

With clear direction in terms of our goal and criteria for decision making, we were ready to get started by taking an energy baseline. We immediately felt the support of our community partnerships when a local engineering firm, Energy Industries, generously performed a comprehensive energy audit. It showed that most of the building's energy was used for two functions: 42% was for lighting and 46% was for air conditioning.

While measuring the energy use provided an economic baseline in terms of the cost of electricity use, and an environmental baseline in terms of the amount of oil used and pollution produced, we needed to find a way to measure the social baseline. The Public Policy Center showed the value of interdisciplinary teamwork by introducing the idea of surveying the community, certainly an idea that was foreign to my engineering training. We learned much about the process of maximizing survey participation. We sent the first survey electronically via email, briefly stating the intent to improve working conditions and saying up front how long the survey would take. (See the Appendix for the full survey.)

We also provided an incentive by offering a prize to the person who guessed closest to Saunders energy use. We then tracked which surveys were still outstanding and sent a follow up email a few days later. Finally at the end of the week, we placed a paper version of the survey in mailboxes of those who had not responded. By reminding outstanding participants every few days for a week we managed to increase the typical participation of 10–30% in such surveys to a whopping 70%.

Interestingly, the number one complaint in the survey was that the air conditioning was too cold, and many also complained that the lights were too bright. Apparently we were spending a lot of money to make people uncomfortable. By identifying community perceptions we expanded the traditional engineering path for addressing what is often viewed as a straight forward technical challenge of reducing an energy bill.

We decided that our first attempt to implement a cumulative increment in the area of energy would be to address the lighting since it was one of the biggest energy users, was unsatisfactory to much of the community and simply seemed more straight forward than the challenge of air conditioning. While there were complaints that the lights were too bright, we knew we had to find a way to measure "too bright" so we could manage it. I happened to be working part time at a local firm called Lighting and Engineering Integrated, and had learned that in Hawaii a City and County Ordinance limits the legal amount of electricity that can be used for buildings based on the square footage, ceiling heights and room usage (Chapter 32: Building Energy Efficiency

Standards, Article 6: Lighting). With software provided by the Department of Business and Economic Development and Tourism (DBEDT), the calculations for Saunders Hall determined that the amount of electricity used for lighting was 44% over the legal limit (Wolfe, 2008, p. 1). We also discovered that the Illuminating Engineering Society (IES) recommends healthy standards for the amount of illumination at a task depending on the type of activity. The units are in footcandles, which is the amount of illumination a birthday candle emits at a distance of one foot.

IES recommended that for typical reading and writing in a classroom 30-50 footcandles would be ideal. Using a Lutron LX-1010b light meter, we found that the typical desk location at Saunders Hall was receiving 120-foot candles from an 8-bulb fixture and 90-foot candles from a 6-bulb fixture, proving that the rooms were indeed over lit (Wolfe, 2008, p. 1). We had succeeded in truly measuring what "too bright" meant and we knew exactly what we wanted to do: reduce Saunders lighting to healthy levels. While straightforward, this insight from our project helped us know where to look to set realistic, measurable goals for each increment. This solidified the following axiom:

Axiom 23: Use professional standards, best practices, and successful case studies to set incremental goals.

After testing various scenarios we identified that removing half of the lamps from every fixture would produce the optimum amount of light. With this technical knowledge, a typical engineering approach would have been to simply notify the departments and begin removing lamps. Yet history had shown that push back from the academic community would be the result, and for good reason. Occupants were accustomed to the light levels, even if they were beyond healthy limits. Community perception that our efforts to reduce the energy bill would cause sacrifice still ran high. If we simply started to remove lamps we would reinforce that false perception.

Our answer was to run a pilot. Simply stated, a pilot is a small scale implementation of a project. It addresses risk aversion since any undesirable effects are small in cost, scale and time frame, and are easily corrected for the next iteration. To be useful, a pilot must also be sufficiently substantial to reveal the benefits and pitfalls of wide-scale implementation. It must be performed with the participation of the community to receive diverse feedback. This also allows measurement beyond economic and environmental factors, and ensures the community benefits, creating an increased triple bottom line. And the more community members who become involved, the more people there will be with experience to advocate for full implementation. Ultimately bugs can be worked out through various iterations until a successful pilot proves the concept.

Axiom 24: Projects start with successful pilots that engage stakeholders and benefit the triple bottom line.

To begin the pilot to remove half the light bulbs in Saunders, we created a one-page document that clearly and simply identified the intention and supporting arguments:

Intention: To bring lighting to healthy levels and increase occupants' health and productivity.

Supporting arguments:

1. the community survey reported dissatisfaction with lighting levels,

2. the light measurements were significantly higher than IES standards,

3. the lighting use was 44% higher than City Ordinance Standards,

4. removing half the lamps would create 30 to 50-foot candles throughout every room and reduce the electricity use to legal standards.

I booked a five-minute meeting with the chair of every department and personally met with them to quickly and efficiently explain our findings. Once they understood, I explained that despite these theoretical findings, we wanted to ensure the new scenario would function well in actuality as well as work out any 'bugs' on a smaller scale before widespread implementation. Pleased with this incremental approach, each department chair agreed to participate, as long as it wouldn't distract their staff from their significant workloads. Anticipating this we had created an email that described the pilot and asked for five volunteers from each floor/department to participate for one month. We clearly identified that a total of only twenty minutes of their time would be needed for de-lamping (removing lamps) and to answer a baseline and follow-up survey to assess the pilot's success.

The chairs were asked to forward this email to their departments with a short personal note requesting those who were interested in participating to contact me directly. With only five minutes of the chair's time we secured top-level approval, and every person in the department was introduced to the concept of de-lamping from their leadership rather than from a new student group. This was in line with Axiom 6: Change starts from top-level leadership. This demonstrated respect, honored path dependency, and avoided putting the faculty in the uncomfortable and time consuming position of trying to decide for themselves if this was a flash-in-the-pan or unfounded effort that might be a waste of their time.

Within a few days we had over thirty volunteers, and nearly five from each floor and department. This ensured that by the end of the pilot, most everyone in the building would have spoken with someone in his or her proximity who had his or her office de-lamped. While it might be surprising, research shows that this might have been the single most important aspect of our efforts for successful wide-scale implementation.

In my favorite book on implementing change, *Fostering Sustainable Behavior*, Dr. Doug McKenzie-Mohr describes this phenomenon through the story of many farmers in the 1930s who were suffering from the loss of vast amounts of topsoil from their fields (McKenzie-Mohr, 2006, p. 33). The US government ran an educational campaign with brochures outlining proven solutions like planting trees as wind screens to reduce the amount of soil being blown away. The entire first chapter of McKenzi-Mohr's book describes how simply giving people information such as brochures rarely works, and this campaign like many others failed to create change. When the government realized nothing was improving, they decided to actually go onto a small farm within a region and physically help them implement the suggestions, creating a pilot that modeled the solutions for other farmers in their area. They hoped the farmers would talk with each other and become familiar enough with the new methods to implement them.

This strategy accomplished what the dry brochures could not: when farmers saw the results they adopted the solutions and the new agricultural practices spread like wildfire. These pilots and social modeling allowed people the opportunity to get comfortable with the new processes at low risk until they no longer seemed new and actually overcame path dependency and risk aversion. With many such case studies it's no wonder that McKenzie-Mohr describes social modeling as one of the most powerful tools for encouraging widespread acceptance of a new concept, process or technology (McKenzie-Mohr, 2006).

This was the case with our Sustainable Saunders de-lamping project. By the time the pilot was complete, every occupant knew what de-lamping was and why it was beneficial to them and the university. They also knew their leadership had vetted and approved the pilot, and since all had been invited to participate there was a sense of inclusion. Once the pilot was deemed successful, the community embraced de-lamping.

In addition to energy use reduction that benefited the economic and environmental bottom line, the pilot proved successful through a survey that showed that headaches, eye strain, and stress decreased, proving an improvement in the social bottom line as shown in figure 3.

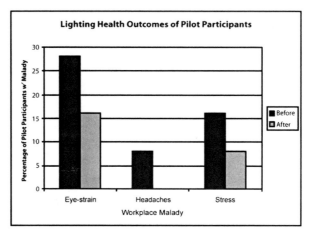

Figure 3: Lighting Health Outcomes of Pilot Participants (Wolfe, 2008, p. 2)

While some participants had been mostly or very dissatisfied with the lighting levels before de-lamping, all were neutral or satisfied with the de-lamped scenarios as shown in Figure 4.

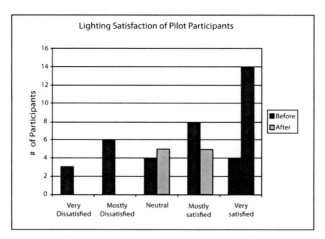

Figure 4: Lighting Satisfaction of Pilot Participants (Wolfe, 2008, p. 2).

With an improvement in the triple bottom line of social, environmental, and economic benefit, the pilot was deemed successful.

The results of the pilot were shared with the community and time was allotted for feedback on the plan to de-lamp all the offices in Saunders Hall. Each student was trained to remove lamps, and also to explain the purpose and pilot results to occupants. We learned that for successful wide-spread implementation, technicians must also be community advocates. Hence the following axiom:

Axiom 25: Implementers are advocates.

De-lampers left a pin-up explanation for present and future occupants with contact information. This created a feedback mechanism for quick corrective action should occupants find the new conditions too dim. With an email or phone call we could quickly bring desk lamps to increase the illumination. Once occupants learned that there would be ongoing communication, they relaxed and accepted trying the change. This feedback loop was key for implementation, so we developed the following axiom:

Axiom 26: Implementation includes follow up.

As a result, only a few occupants requested that their lamps be returned. Nearly 2,000 lamps were removed from Saunders Hall, bringing lighting levels into legal and healthy limits and saving the University $15,000 a year without spending a cent.

We had charted a course that accomplished for the first time a widespread energy-saving implementation without pushback in Saunders Hall. But would the process work for other projects? It was time to tackle the air conditioning and we followed the same Axioms to allow the path to emerge. First, recognizing that change must build on existing efforts, we needed to determine what the facilities engineers had attempted or deemed ideal.

We discovered that the air conditioning was designed for the worst-case scenario: a hot day, at noon, and with a room full of people contributing their body heat to the space. As an engineer I could completely sympathize with this strategy of ensuring the worst conditions would be cooled. With a very limited number of engineers to run the entire campus due to an ever-decreasing facilities budget, they did not have the time or the means to measure variability throughout the day and had received complaints when they had tried turning the air conditioning off on previous occasions. The engineers were very supportive of attempting to reduce the air conditioning on an incremental basis if we could liaison with the community to avoid the pushback they so often had to deal with. This perfectly satisfied our belief that slow, cumulative changes make consistent progress.

A chance element came along when the air conditioning had to be shut down for routine maintenance. As the community already accepted these shut-downs, this was our opportunity to gauge the resulting temperature in the building. We placed wireless sensors called HOBO buttons that read the temperature and humidity every minute in various rooms. Once we downloaded the data collected we were able to identify how the temperature changed throughout the day when the air conditioning was turned off.

We identified that when the air conditioning was off, the building stayed cool for the morning, evening and nighttime, and was much warmer during the daytime hours. When the air conditioning was on, the temperature was hitting the engineers' goal of around 72 degrees Fahrenheit mid-day, but it was much colder in the mornings, evening and nighttime. Timed air conditioning shut downs were the answer.

While we originally strove to ensure temperatures did not dip below 72 degrees, we researched where this standard might have come from. A local company, Island Controls, sponsored another student, Vance Arakaki, and I to attend in-depth air conditioning training. Vance had worked with his family's construction company most of his life and had been on a trajectory to be a general contractor. When he discovered the HUB he also discovered that, while he specialized in construction, he was pulled to learn as much about the big picture as possible so he could be a part of systemic change.

Vance and I were stoked to learn all we could about how air conditioning could make a big impact on systemically reducing the campus's energy use. We were both surprised to learn that air conditioning levels should correspond to the amount of clothing someone is wearing, which is actually quantified by a unit of measure called CLO. For example, someone wearing a business suit has a CLO of 1 and prefers 72 degrees, which is why most air conditioning aims for that temperature. Interestingly, women would score a lower CLO unit if they wore skirts. Yet air conditioning across the country was apparently set for a man's suit. And in Hawaii most people wear aloha shirts, shorts and sandals, which are quantified by a CLO of 0.5 and should prefer 76 degrees. We confirmed this theory at Saunders by taking temperature readings throughout the building. A third of the occupants could control their own air conditioners, and we found that they kept their rooms at an average of 76 degrees confirming the theory. Again, we had used professional standards, best practices, and successful case studies to set a realistic, measurable goal of 76 degrees.

Once we had a goal in place, a pilot was performed. We decided that the incremental changes would begin in the nighttime hours from midnight to 5am with this window increasing slowly, gauging community acceptance at each level. Had we simply turned off the air conditioning at the level we thought optimum, there might have been pushback and no intervals would have been implemented. In this way each increment accepted by the community would be an irreversible step toward the end goal of maximum shut down time.

As in the de-lamping pilot, the community was engaged and we wanted to ensure that the triple bottom line would benefit. Notifications were sent from Facilities to all building secretaries, who in turn informed their departments about each increment of air conditioning reduction. The HUB email address was provided so that we could field all feedback and liaison between the community and Facilities. Occupants quickly understood and seemed to appreciate that we were going to test increasing lengths of air conditioning elimination, and that they could directly give their feedback and participate in identifying the optimal length. While the community's response via email let us know when occupants were not satisfied, the electricity meter on the building showed how much electricity and pollution was reduced. Since implementation includes follow up, this feedback mechanism for the community again invited and allowed ALL to participate so there was no pushback and the optimal level of air conditioning shut-downs was determined.

Following the axioms with these two changes alone, the Sustainable Saunders Initiative was able to bring occupancy comfort into healthy levels and reduce the building's energy use by 24%, saving $150,000 annually—all without spending a cent. Our measureable success spread like wildfire as I was asked to present our methodology at events, conferences, business meetings, schools, and organizations all over Hawaii. Everyone was looking for ways to save money in tight times with record high electricity rates and we were soon front-page news. We were no longer a cute student group rallying for positive change; we were credible implementers with a valuable process that could put money into home and business owner's pockets across the state.

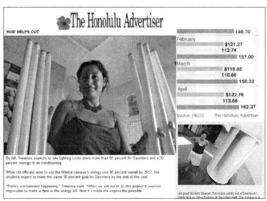

Chapter 9

Replicating Change

While accomplishing such triple bottom line success so quickly might seem the pinnacle of our efforts, the good times had only just begun. The campus finally had the proof of concept needed to implement de-lamping and air conditioning shut downs on a widespread scale, much as they had always wanted to do. The Sea Grant Program and the Center for Smart Building and Community Design created a lighting audit program where hired student interns began performing lighting audits across campus. Facilities began asking buildings to volunteer for 'Manoa Green Days,' which meant that on designated holidays, weekends and evenings, participating buildings would have their air conditioning turned off.

This ripple effect was just what we had hoped for, but the extent and longevity was far more than we could have imagined. We were overwhelmed at the supportive response from the campus and inspired when other organizations began contacting us to collaborate. We joined forces with the Architecture Sustainability Lab to do an energy audit of our campus's largest building,

Hamilton Library, and identified $700,000 in similar no-cost saving. We also worked with the Engineers without Borders to design a water catchment system, Net Impact from the Business School to host panel discussions, and threw lunch party recycling drives with the Geology Club and Grounds and Landscaping.

A great example of our creative collaborations occurred in one my favorite areas, food. Food is big love of most students, so we were excited to meet the regional president of our main food service provider, Sodexo, and learn that he was a sustainability supporter. He was trying to introduce Styrophobia, a local vendor of biodegradable cups, plates and cutlery, on campus and was planning a pilot in an all-you-can-eat dorm cafeteria. Since Sustainable Saunders had a good track record of engaging students, the campus and the press, we offered to help bring some excitement and hype to the pilot to foster support that could lead to widespread implementation. Rather than just one initiative we suggested a comprehensive 'greening' of the cafeteria that would bring in more media and also address some challenges we had unearthed the previous year.

We had completed a waste audit of the five main campus food service providers and found that over 55% of the waste had been organic material including food and discarded drinks. This 'plate waste' was a concern; we had spent a lot of money and energy to get the food to the most remote population center in the world, only to have much of it dumped into the garbage. Tamara Armstrong, an Environmental Studies Major who had led the waste audit, suggested removing the trays from the cafeteria so people might think twice about taking food they don't want. Previously other campuses had found a 35% reduction in plate waste and a 25% reduction in water use from no longer needing to wash trays.

As we found with most departments, Sodexo was well aware of such options, but justifiably feared pushback from their customers. Imagine coming to your cafeteria after an intense exam only to find no more trays. Chaos might ensue, so we decided to be creative and collaborate instead. Tamara led the HUB in planting flowers in biodegradable cups, creating centerpieces for all the cafeteria tables. Using markers, they drew graffiti messages onto the cups describing how they were made from potatoes not plastic and other relevant facts.

Campus DJs set up their decks at the front of the cafeteria and a dozen HUB members wearing t-shirts printed with our motto 'Sustainability is Sexy' handed out free organic cake. It was a party, and as the HUB interacted with the students they got  the message across about the benefits of going biodegradable and tray-less. Students were further engaged as Tamara asked questions between music sets about the facts printed on every table. Freshmen ran to the front with their answers to win t-shirts and other prizes. The event was a success, not only because we made four television news channels that night, but because, rather than feeling sacrifice, all the students that day felt part of something worthwhile.

Going tray-less is now a trend that Sodexo continues to roll out across campus, offsetting the slightly higher price of the biodegradable tableware. Tamara Armstrong has since graduated and was hired by an architecture firm, KYA Design Group. Two of the original previously mentioned HUB members, Vance Arakaki, a business major, and Sean Connelly, an architect, were also hired, and the three were tasked with creating one of Hawaii's first sustainability focused consulting firms, KYA Sustainability Studio (see photo next page). Their first project? Performing a waste audit and creating a comprehensive recycling and waste management program for Honolulu Airport.

We also fostered unique collaborations every semester by hosting a public forum where spectators quickly became participants. Large round tables were labeled with areas of interest such as 'Recycling', 'Energy Efficiency', or 'Cycling' and everyone in attendance self-organized around their topic of interest. Using a presentation of our latest projects as fodder for discussion, each table work-shopped ideas that could be implemented in their area of interest at their building or in the campus community.

At our first workshop an Urban Planning student, HUB member and avid cyclist, Daniel Alexander, hosted a group of random faculty, administration and students at the 'Bicycling' table. A couple of hours later, a new organization was born that would change campus transport for years to come. Named Cycle Manoa, the group used the HUB logo, adding spokes to create a bicycle wheel, and modified the HUB 3-word 'Live, Connect, Create' motto to 'Educate, Advocate, Ride.' Meeting weekly, the campus bicyclists formed UH's first bicycle community by going on an hour-long ride before holding a strategy meeting, led in the collaborative spirit of the HUB. They worked with Facilities to transform some empty warehouse space at the fringe of campus into a bike shop where they teach students how to be bike mechanics. Facilities also delivers all the abandoned bikes left on campus at the end of each semester so they can be fixed up for Cycle Manoa's hugely popular 'Bike-buy-back' sales. This revenue stream is used to buy tools and parts for the 'Kick-Stand', a free mobile bike-repair clinic set up at different locations around campus.

Cycle Manoa is working with the Transport Department to bring the first car share program to Hawaii. Students and faculty will be able to use their smart phones to unlock a hybrid car on campus, and will pay around $9 an hour, which includes gas and insurance, to do everything from errands to go surfing. And not only do they accomplish all these incredible projects, they have a lot of fun doing what they love — riding. If you're ever in Hawaii, sign up for their island ride, which goes all around the perimeter of each island, camping included.

It was exciting to see so many unique collaborative projects repeatedly prove successful, but a whole new approach to widespread replication emerged with the vision of another inspired student leader. Amy Brinker was born in a small Texas town and at the age of nineteen moved to Oahu after living on Galveston Island near Houston where she fell  in love with surfing. Though she had a background in culinary arts, after moving to Hawaii Amy took an interest in Hawaiian culture, which eventually led her to the Richardson School of Law specializing in Native Hawaiian issues. Within her first two years Amy proved herself a notable campus sustainability leader as she simultaneously launched action on many diverse fronts. As Vice President of the Student Bar Association (SBA), she was the first organization officer to approach Sustainable Saunders and recommend an expansion to consult with other student groups.

Sustainable Richardson was born and the HUB spent a year visiting the Law School weekly to perform waste, energy and water audits, creating a working model for expansion of the program —

all while helping the SBA move toward their goal of being the greenest Law School in America. While she proved her abilities as an auditor and organizational leader, Amy simultaneously incorporated her culinary arts and legal training to work on cultural sustainability and food sovereignty issues.

She found out about a Department of Health (DOH) prohibition on the sale of *pa'i 'ai*, which is traditionally pounded *poi* (mashed *taro* root) before it has been diluted with water. Although this was once the staple food of Hawaii, the DOH deemed *pa'i 'ai* unsanitary when a young man started a business to produce and sell it. She recognized that the DOH had not intentionally promulgated the regulations for the specific purpose of prohibiting traditional food preparation; rather, they had adopted food code guidelines from the federal government that viewed the pounding tools unsanitary and did not have Hawaiian culture in mind.

Knowing the paramount significance of *pa'i 'ai* to the social, mental, physical, and spiritual health of Kānaka Maoli, Hawaii's indigenous population, Amy began a journey to not only legalize the sale of traditionally pounded *poi*, but to use the issue as an inaugural effort to indigenize laws, starting at the local level with the goal of making an impact on Federal law. From her 'Legalize Pa'i 'ai' bumper sticker campaign to her indigenizethelaw.com website, Amy is building a movement around cultural sustainability in Hawaii by bringing awareness to the need to adapt laws to reflect localized and indigenous cultures.

Amy was a powerful change agent on campus not only because of her insights and ideas, but because she was able to engage her community. For example, she invited Catherine Bye, a librarian at the Law Library who was a green enthusiast, to help. We learned that the law library staff toured the library every hour to record information about cubicle use, so we worked with them to extend their hourly data collection to all the rooms in the law school. They recorded whether the lights were on or off and the number of people in each room every hour between

8am and 11pm for a two-week period. We found that the there were nearly 8,000 hours per year in which the lights are on with no one occupying a room. If occupancy sensors ensured lights were out in empty rooms, nearly $3,000 would be saved annually, reducing lighting electricity use by nearly 9%. If a policy was instituted that required a minimum of three people in each classroom, effectively creating 'room pooling' in the spirit of car pooling, the amount the Law School would save nearly doubled to $6,000 annually or 17% of the lighting bill, making occupancy sensors even more economically viable.

Sustainable Saunders continued to create other chapters by making weekly visits to other campuses in the UH system like our first at Honolulu Community College (HCC), where we collaborated to create Sustainable HCC. Our efforts continued to be recognized, which earned me a position on the selection committee for the next President of the University System. In collaboration with the HUB I introduced a new goal for the next President's efforts on campus: to cultivate the University of Hawaii System as a world leader in sustainable education, research, and practices. While there had been only seven Presidential goals for years, the Board of Regents unanimously passed this eighth goal and finally we knew that even at the system level the change we desired was valued. Again a bridge between grassroots and upper administration had been formed. Beyond UHM's campus, there was now alignment with the direction from top-level leadership and the growing efforts throughout the system.

While we were just one small group of students, through each collaboration a new project was born that could never have been accomplished by us alone. It also opened doors we couldn't have dreamed of. It was the synergy of different perspectives, voices, interests, and skill sets that turned individuals and groups into networks. And it was the excitement of the process, the rush of creating something meaningful and new, and the fun spirit in which we worked and played together that turned our networks into a movement.

CHAPTER 10

Engaging Everyone

Since we had expanded beyond Saunders Hall and into the UH system, we needed a new name for our organization and after much brainstorming we decided on Sustainable UH. As I had participated in interviews for UH Presidential candidates, one thing stood out from the nation's campus leaders: they didn't want surprises. They depended on their staff to let them know what was going on so they could make informed decisions. So we booked meetings with the administration including the Chancellor to share our new direction. We wanted to share our new mission statement: to be of service to all those establishing the UH system as a world leader in sustainable education, research, and practices. By beginning our mission with the intent to 'be of service' and concluding with our intent to support top-level priorities, we hoped that our effort to expand would not be perceived as an effort to dictate change throughout the system, but that we would be available to anyone who wished to create positive change in line with the system's goals. Yet this name change still spawned mixed responses. We received emails in the tone of 'who do you think you are.' One email even said that we were spreading like a cancer without thought of whose toes we might be stepping on.

A campus faculty who we had repeatedly tried to reach but would not return our calls finally called me to his office once he saw our public announcement. He warned against my crusade to take over campus leadership, promote for my personal fame and gain, and co-opt students with my charisma. Thinking of Axiom 3, remember those who oppose you are human too, I listened carefully and then suggested a different perspective. All our projects had been created in response to requests from the community and not by me, and I had left a successful career to be a student myself. So if I cared about my personal gain I would have kept my top-level management position and matching salary. I told him that the whole team had wonderful charisma and invited him to come meet everyone any time. I thanked him for sharing his perspective and listening to mine. Using Axiom 2, where finding common ground can diffuse opposing viewpoints, I commented that since we were both obviously passionate about how sustainability was getting implemented on campus, I hoped we could bridge and work together soon. Later, I was thrilled at our Sustainable UH launch event when I saw him sitting in the audience. He had taken my offer that evening, and continued to attend all our public meetings going forward. He is now one of our most consistent collaborators and one of our greatest champions, both on and off campus.

It took years to prove that we were something beyond a flash-in-the-pan student group full of good ideas but nothing to show for it. I am happy to say that four years into the program most known 'ripples of resistance' have turned into supportive collaborators. Our proof of concepts earned us the reputation of turning ideas into action, and today our projects and partnerships emerge smoothly and implementation gets easier and easier as the campus and community culture continues to evolve and embrace change.

Again, this movement began as a hope and an intention. While we were devoted to goals, we were operating with many moving parts so we had to be flexible and responsive. As such, we committed to valuing the process over the destination creating the following axiom:

Axiom 27: Let the path emerge.

This recognizes that just being willing to take a step in the right direction would reveal the next step. It also acknowledges that the path to a destination is rarely known and linear in the real world. One of my Planning professors drove this home when he told us of a chat he had shared with an airplane pilot at a dinner party. He had asked the pilot how often he was off-course as he flew toward a destination. Our professor then asked the class what we thought the pilot's answer was and we threw out 12%, 30%, maybe 45%. The pilot had said it was typical to be off-course about 97% of the time! Apparently being off course was a very natural part of getting to where you want to go. Not only did it make logistical sense, it was part of the process we enjoyed the most. It was exciting to move with the momentum. If people wanted a bike shop, we went that way and enjoyed the ride. We created a network of interlocking interests that kept moving outwards instead of trying to accomplish rigid predetermined goals. This philosophy negated the need to have everything figured out before hand, and a larger movement than we could have ever mapped out was created.

Part of being off-course is that sometimes errors or mistakes are made. There were many times we thought an activity was a valuable next step, when it proved to be a distraction. Sometimes we just plain messed up. After every event and initiative we held a debriefing session where we invited stakeholders to provide feedback. We were told that we had forgotten to place signs on campus leading the way to Earth Day, we had left posters up months after an event, we neglected to invite some stakeholders to a discussion, or perhaps forgot to thank important supporters as I probably did at the beginning of this book … our errors were endless. Yet, rather than be paralyzed by fear of making a mistake, we did our best and learned from our errors. There were many unexpected successes and failures, and we learned from them all according to one of our most loved axioms:

Axiom 28: Accountability turns mistakes into lessons.

We thanked everyone for their feedback and sincerely strove to make improvements. This addressed risk aversion, which can be thought of as the fear of failure, by repositioning failure as a necessary and positive step for growth. Accountability also made us respectable partners resulting in all the collaborations that are the foundation of our success.

To return the respect and to honor our partners, we never forgot the first advice we received from a top campus administrator when the initiative began:

Axiom 29: Give away credit whenever possible.

This wasn't intended to stroke egos to foster more collaboration, but to sincerely honor often unrecognized efforts. This fostered a sense of community and ensured that we never lost sight of the true strength of our progress. The deep interconnection of everyone working for change was like many teacups that together could douse the house on fire and combined put out the flames of a burning building.

Over four years we built a movement, engaged previously opposing stakeholders, built community, and inspired and excited everyone toward change. And we were just students. As the stakeholders who historically had the least power, we had somehow become empowered to be the change agents that catalyzed a cultural transformation on campus.

In writing this book I finally had an opportunity to reflect on just how this had happened. How had I not known a single soul in Hawaii and four years later many just like me had become powerful change agents? I set out to explore the process of empowerment.

CHAPTER 11

Empowering the Powerless as Change Leaders

I first looked to Urban Planning to see how this profession viewed empowerment. Interestingly, I found that empowerment at the community level has historically been a solution accepted by both the political left and right in planning, hence an important common ground (Rocha, 1997, p. 31). While empowerment means different things in varying fields, in planning it tends to encompass community participation and grassroots coalitions created to provide goods and services, all of which are applicable to the structure and goals of the Sustainable Saunders initiative. To attempt to categorize power, Sherry Arnstein, a public policy analyst in the late 1960s, constructed a ladder of citizen participation, which she likened to citizen power. She stated that, "It is the redistribution of power that enables the have-not citizens, presently excluded from the political and economic processes, to be deliberately included in the future." (Arnstein, 1969, p. 2). Figure 5 shows the rungs of this ladder.

Early top-down Planners such as Robert Moses would align with the lower nonparticipation rungs since they openly manipulated and imposed plans without citizen participation. Subsequent planning models strove to move up the rungs to partnership, but often fell short and were criticized for tokenism. While modern participatory processes strive to create citizen power, the Sustainable UH initiative demonstrated a true proof of concept since it was the usual 'have-nots', the students or citizens, who were the power behind implementing change. It was clear by this model's categorization that we had achieved the highest level of citizen power. Yet I still wondered how?

Three decades after Arnstein created her ladder, a Planning professor at the University of Oregon, Elizabeth Rocha, set out to answer the question: What is empowerment? Her answer built on Arnstein's theory when she created the Ladder of Empowerment shown in Figure 6.

The lowest rung focuses on the individual as the locus of empowerment, with each rung

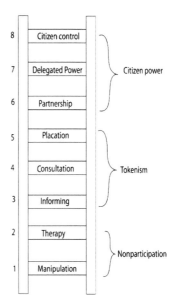

Figure 5: Arnstein's Ladder of Citizen Participation (Arnstein, 1969, p. 4)

Figure 6: A Ladder of Empowerment (Rocha, 1997, p. 34)

increasing toward community as the locus. The first thing I noticed was that aspects of Sustainable UH fostered empowerment at all levels. Rung 1 occurs when individuals feel empowered in their ability to feel personal satisfaction. This individualized empowerment occurs in the HUB when students identify and are supported in pursuing their individual passion and curiosity.

Rung 2 empowerment is defined as the empowerment that occurs when individuals expand their personal satisfaction through structured involvement. As they socialize in an organizational setting such as Sustainable UH their empowerment increases beyond what they could experience by simply being by themselves. Mediation empowerment occurs for individuals when they connect with others in a professional sense or by taking moralized action. Students experienced mediation empowerment when they contacted vendors, politicians, manufacturers and all sorts of partners and collaborators through our events and projects. This empowerment stays with them when they graduate into careers and feel confident in building business relationships.

For example, David 'Tamba' Aquino and Ivory McClintock were both born and raised in Hawaii and had held part time jobs at various restaurants and retail stores. When they joined Sustainable UH they found their pull in bringing events together. Tamba excelled at project management from setting up a comprehensive network of signs to direct thousands to our events to leading teams of energy auditors to collect and crunch data. Ivory proved to be an incredible community organizer and could lead volunteers in everything from setting up a hundred Earth Day tents to moderating workshops. They caught the eye of a local non-profit organization called Blue Planet Foundation, whose intention is to rid the world of fossil-fuel use starting with Hawaii. Blue Planet sent them to Washington D.C. to represent them at the 2009 Power Shift event. They were impressed with their confidence and ability to organize the other students as well as speak with high-level politicians about complex issues. As a result, after graduating, Tamba and Ivory moved out of their restaurant and retail jobs and now work for Blue Planet: Tamba as an Energy Project Manager and Ivory as their Outreach Coordinator.

The higher levels of empowerment also emerged from the initiative. The Socio-Political Empowerment fourth rung level, also called 'transformative populism', places the community as the locus of power and emphasizes the need for collaborative social action to promote growth (Rocha, 1997, p. 37). At this level, the organization is the mechanism through which the individual AND the community become empowered (Rocha, 1997, p. 38). This is reflective of Sustainable UH, in which individuals and organizations across campus and throughout Hawaii were able to leverage the organization's momentum and proof of concepts to empower their own initiatives, by either collaborating or using our successes as proof of concepts. As they referenced us to gain power, we in turn gained power, much as an author repeatedly cited gains credibility.

The HUB of Sustainable Saunders climbed to the fifth rung of 'Political Empowerment' when we introduced a Bill into the Legislative Session of 2009. Rocha explains that a community has entered the fifth rung of Political Empowerment when it is competing for resources, which in turn empowers the community (Rocha, 1997, p. 39). The HUB had asked for a portion of the energy savings we had participated in creating to be returned to our organization for subsequent projects so that we could create an internship program called RISE (Rewarding Internships for Sustainable Employment). The money would pay student interns to replicate Saunders successes throughout the campus and would leverage community funds as businesses and organizations hired interns through the program. If we could create an internship program where students could replace their entry level part time jobs with meaningful experiences that would build their confidence and resumes and allow them to network with potential employers, then we would be building rewarding, well paying career paths for our passionate students, as well as building our local economy. But we needed funds for mentors, administration and equipment, hence we requested the energy savings. Our requests were repeatedly denied on the grounds that the Facilities budget was already grossly underfunded.

Unwilling to remain powerless in creating a program we believed in, we worked to introduce a bill through our Interactive Launch Party with political supporters we had engaged three years previously. We requested $200,000 to create the RISE program and many students testified passionately. The bill received unanimous support from all four committees in the House and Senate until it died in the final Ways and Means Committee. While the funds were not won, we still gained empowerment by Rocha's definition since the process engendered recognition and respect for the values, members, and leaders of the oppressed group, in this case the HUB (Rocha, 1997, p. 40). And when stimulus funding came to the state a few months later, our program was top of mind as an ideal candidate and was finally assigned funding.

Additionally as a result of these efforts, the Sustainable Saunders Initiative was honored with a House Resolution on March 11, 2010 that recognized our successes and offered continued encouragement from the Legislature. We could not have forseen that our efforts would result in statewide political support. Nonetheless, taking a step we truly believed in without knowing the outcome had brought us time and time again many unforseen rewards in the form of collaborations, funding, awareness and opportunities. Most importantly, what the subsequent steps should be had also emerged.

We had done this for years, knowing that for such wicked problems we could only see so far toward the horizon. The complexity and the many components involved in systemic change were impossible to simultaneously comprehend. With each step we did not know what would come next, but we knew it would take us in the right direction guided by our proven axioms. And, indeed, the next step always became obvious.

It would be nice to say that the emergence of the next step was always graceful with door after door opening, but sometimes our next step was revealed because door after door slammed shut. This was especially the case of finding a home for the RISE program. We needed a department that would take in the funds from the internship employer and hire the students. For many reasons ranging from not having enough staff to disinterest in internships, department after department turned down our request. While large bureaucracies are so often criticized for their complexity and size, we found these attributes to be the greatest assets when we realized we had what seemed like infinite options within the ten campus system. If we were not valued in one location we didn't need to convert them. This would have been a push, and we operated by pull. If they were not pulled by the RISE program, we didn't take it personally and simply went in search of who did.

In the meantime we knew that projects start with successful pilots, so we worked with the Public Policy Center to pilot the program once with only two interns. This would not overstretch their thin resources for an extended period, but would help us demonstrate the proof of concept. Sarah Rosen, a sociology student and Michelle Cosky, an engineering student worked together to perform a waste audit of the U.S. Coast Guard Sand Island Base. Their recommendations for recycling, compost, and bulky item disposal would save the Coast Guard $16,000 annually. The Coast Guard became familiar with their abilities and the interns grew in value as they learned more and more about the Coast Guard and the Base. As we had hoped, following their internships both students were hired full time to perform energy audits. The pilot saved resources and money, while fostering a conscious culture for the Coast Guard and creating new green jobs. With the triple bottom line benefiting, the pilot was deemed a success.

After many closed doors on UHM's campus in our search for a home for the program, we decided to approach college campuses that were more focused on workforce development. We started with HCC since we already had relationships through our collaboration with Sustainable HCC. They appreciated the proof of concept from our successful pilot and agreed to house the program. Our second, larger pilot was for the head of Facilities for the statewide Department of Education (DOE). A six-member team representing architecture, engineering, urban planning, international business, economics, and political science performed a sustainability assessment of a K-6 school. The assessment included water, energy, and waste audits, as well as an Energy Star assessment, solar analysis, and education displays and workshops for all age groups at the school (see the Appendix for complete methodology).

The team identified $85,000 in no-to-low-cost savings and the DOE was pleased, immediately seeing how the recommendations could be implemented at similar schools across the state. And the benefits extended even beyond the DOE. The interns created education modules and we partnered with Blue Planet Foundation, who pays the interns to train other groups on how to perform what we call 'educational sustainability assessments' in fun, interactive workshops. The interns give an hour-long training session and then the group breaks into teams to perform three hours of assessing. For the last hour everyone comes back together to brainstorm recommendations, and then we celebrate with some good food. Our model of 'learning by doing' not only allows more buildings to become sustainable, as people are engaged along the way, the culture of energy literacy throughout our communities is ever increasing.

Our successes ultimately led to a result that was beyond what we had hoped for. The system office that oversees all the college campuses took an interest in the program and now houses it at one of the highest levels possible, making internship opportunities available to all campuses in the system. Because we kept going when each door closed and viewed the large bureaucrocy as endless potential, we finally found the ideal home where we could be most easily accessed and make the biggest impact. This solidified the final axiom for our efforts:

Axiom 30: Keep going!

There is always someone who will value you and what you have to offer. Bureaucracies, your community, and the world are big enough that if one door closes you need not take it personally or consider it a burned bridge. The closed door is still part of your network, much like a HUB member who does not feel the pull to work on your *kuleana* with you is still your team mate. There is someone else who is a better fit for your collaboration, so just keep going.

Through this unique way of allowing the path to emerge in due time and finding collaborators along the way while considering everyone a team mate, the HUB gained power not through the usual means of occupying an established position in the institution or raising funds, but by connecting and collaborating as comprehensively as possible. By fully participating with each other, other organizations, and the academic and political arenas, we fostered citizen power as described in Arnstein's Ladder. Our unique culture ensured that individuals, organizations, and institutions representing all rungs in Rocha's ladder of empowerment were engaged in the process of change and felt empowered by it. By sharing power, by recognizing it in everyone, and by giving it away, we gained it.

CHAPTER 12

A New Model for Change

The previous chapters show how axioms revealed through our movement building on campus proved to be a useful framework for many diverse challenges. But do they offer a new model for change? An exploration of the history of planning theory sheds light on the uniqueness of this model.

Throughout its entire history, one of the major reasons each model of planning evolved was to attempt new ways of grappling with top-down and bottom-up stakeholders, all with the goal of serving the public good. As the limits of rational top-down planning were revealed, more human-centered 'advocacy planning' processes arose. While they attempted to advocate and plan for the disenfranchised, they did not include them as participants in the process and left the top-down power structure intact (Sandercock, 1998, p. 90). This was akin to Facilities planning with students, faculty and staff in mind, but not including them in the process.

This model still left me disappointed. As a student ready for action, being designed for, rather than doing the designing, was completely unsatisfactory. Other models such as 'radical planning' pit those in power as the enemy, and somewhat glorified community action as doing no wrong (Sandercock, 1998, p. 101). Radical planning applied to the campus would give students and faculty all the power and would dismiss the usefulness of Facilities or Administration, which has often been the strategy in the history of student groups. Political Science students at UHM had riled against the power structure in many protests and, while impressed by their vigor, when I asked if they had been successful in any of their endeavors, I most often heard the answer 'no.' Changing the power from top-up to bottom-down certainly hadn't been our solution.

I eventually learned of the first model that incorporated the disenfranchised such as students in a collaborative planning process with top-down stakeholders. Formed in the early 1980s it was called the Social Learning and Communicative Action Model since it emerged in an attempt to evolve planning by involving bottom-up players. No longer was the planner the only participant with expertise. Local and experiential knowledge of the community became of value and planning was viewed as an interactive, communicative activity (Sandercock, 1998, p. 95-96).

Yet I soon realized that while the Communicative Action Model is perhaps the most useful known model for collaborative multi-stakeholder processes, it still prioritized the formally educated planner working primarily through those in power (Sandercock, 1998, p. 87). This centralized control seemed the core of the problem, since in real life challenges there cannot be one person or manager with complete overview (Van Assche & Verschraegen, 2008, p. 280). Since there is not a center to planning, and it is instead systemic, there should be an interconnection of roles, not one focal planning role.

The HUB considered our efforts as part of a system where each group was respected for their individual strengths rather than a hierarchy. We could each rise to leadership depending on the project, and collaborate on some level on nearly all projects. So much more could be accomplished this way! Yet this perspective did not seem to show up in planning theory. While all the models through urban planning history offered beneficial aspects to multi-stakeholder collaborative planning, none offered a comprehensive, systemic approach with distributed, shared leadership and control.

Society, including myself as a student ready for action on campus, was in great need of a new model based on new theory. Renowned Australian planning theorist, Leonie Sandercock, noted that the role of the planner in all existing models was either aligned with those in power or with a community that opposes those in power, leaving the dialectical relationship between those in power and the mobilized community unexplored (Sandercock, 1998, p. 102). She called for the same model that we had created: an exploration of social and institutional transformation as a result of the impact from mobilized top-down and bottom-up groups working as a network rather than a hierarchy.

She further recommended that leadership to overcome the tensions between bottom-up and top-down perspectives could come from marginalized groups such as women and people of color who have experienced marginality, exploitation, and domination (Sandercock, 1998, p. 102). From her perspective, the disenfranchised that were not politically or economically entrenched and had built tools to deal with oppressive processes could be the ones to create common ground for all stakeholders, just as we had experienced! In the case of the campus, this would mean that the students, who had historically felt frustrated and powerless, were best positioned to lead the way to change. One of the greatest strengths of students is that we are politically and financially independent from most power structures. Our job and our income do not rely on conforming to status quo beliefs. And, most importantly, when we set out to find answers we have no overt or hidden agenda. We are ultimately looking for education in the form of solutions.

In the hundred-year history of urban planning, no model has embraced the disenfranchised in order to create common ground to dispel top-down and bottom-up tension, effectively building a bridge and uniting these forces into a power-sharing network for change. Yet as students working with the academic community and facilities, this is exactly the model we proved viable.

Together the axioms we forged through Sustainable Saunders and Sustainable UH at the University of Hawaii form their own model that I call TEM (Transformative Emergent Model). It is a synergy of many previous urban planning models with theory from Futures and other disciplines, as well as emergent principles identified through the HUB dynamic that together create a unique form of empowerment for the individuals, the organization and the community. In the area of urban planning TEM reflects aspects of Equity Planning where the role of the planner is to consciously redistribute power, resources, or participation. It also differs from this model, which retains a belief in the planners' expertise and does not draw on local knowledge (Sandercock, 1998, p. 43).

TEM could be considered a Social Learning and Communicative Action Model since it honors local and experiential knowledge, planning as a communicative practice, mutual learning, and action (Sandercock, 1998, p. 45). However, the Communicative Action Model has been criticized for failing to incorporate the 'peculiar political and professional nuances' that exist in the applied experience (Tewdwr-Jones & Allmendinger, 1998, p. 1975), which the TEM addresses through the axioms that arose from real life projects. The Communicative Action Model still maintains the formally educated planner as the primary director and focus of process working through those in power (Sandercock, 1998, p. 87), where TEM distributes both leadership and power.

TEM does not fit the Radical Planning model, which strives to reverse polarizations by pitting those in power as the enemy, and glorifying community action as doing no wrong (Sandercock,

1998, p. 101). TEM provides tools for creating collaborative relationships between those in top-level positions and the mobilized community, and empowers all including the disenfranchised. Just as Sandercock had advocated, the guidance to address the tensions between state-directed and grassroots efforts comes from marginalized groups (Sandercock, 1998, p. 87). Through its many unique traits, the TEM framework offers something unique to planning processes everywhere.

The following summarizes the key elements of the TEM model:

1. the challenge is acknowledged as a 'wicked' problem, with complexity and uncertainty rendering centralized master planning of little use;

2. the end goal is not a master plan, but rather an overarching vision of a preferred future;

3. the end goals represent a transformative future;

4. rather than being predetermined, the path emerges from path dependent factors and incorporating chance occurrences;

5. pilots and slow irreversible incremental steps overcome risk aversion and liability concerns;

6. power comes from the previously disenfranchised, serving as a "bridge" or community liaison between polarized top-down and bottom-up efforts;

7. all levels, including individual, community, and political arenas, are empowered through the organization applying TEM.

In review, the TEM Axioms are as follows:

Axiom 1: Every challenge can be turned into an opportunity.

Axiom 2: Replace tensions with bridges.

Axiom 3: Remember those who oppose you are human too.

Axiom 4: Coalitions do not mean compromising values.

Axiom 5: Coalitions collaborate on common ground.

Axiom 6: Change starts with clear direction from top-level leadership.

Axiom 7: Grassroots change is more likely to succeed if it accomplishes top-level priorities.

Axiom 8: Passion + Positive Action = Effective Change Agent.

Axiom 9: Diversity + Interdisciplinary = Creative Solutions.

Axiom 10: Optimal Experience = Effective Change Agent.

Axiom 11: Keep raising the bar to continually create optimal experiences.

Axiom 12: Pull not Push = Team Stamina.

Axiom 13: Working together keeps things on track.

Axiom 14: Meetings are for creative, collaborative problem solving.

Axiom 15: Change must build on existing efforts.

Axiom 16: Slow, cumulative changes make consistent progress.

Axiom 17: Each increment must move irreversibly toward the end goal.

Axiom 18: Incorporate 'wild cards' in line with your overarching goals.

Axiom 19: Initial projects must be highly visible and widely accessible.

Axiom 20: You can't manage what you don't measure.

Axiom 21: An overarching goal must inspire change.

Axiom 22: Each step must benefit the triple bottom line.

Axiom 23: Use professional standards, best practices, and successful case studies to set incremental goals.

Axiom 24: Projects start with successful pilots that engage stakeholders and benefit the triple bottom line.

Axiom 25: Implementers are advocates.

Axiom 26: Implementation includes follow up.

Axiom 27: Let the path emerge.

Axiom 28: Accountability turns mistakes into lessons.

Axiom 29: Give away credit whenever possible.

Axiom 30: Keep going!

PART 3
Riding the Waves

Chapter 13

The Business Case for Change

While the TEM axioms proved useful in many of our diverse efforts, we were inspired along the way by those who were using similar guiding philosophies to implement change in other arenas. Many of us possessed entrepreneurial spirits and had long looked up to Ray Anderson, a business leader who was featured in the documentary, "The Corporation". In fact, while viewing a film with this corporate champion of sustainability in sixth grade, an original HUB member, Tamara Armstrong, was so inspired that she knew she had found her calling. Through his bravery and success in using the triple bottom line to guide his company from one of the most polluting and energy intensive in the world, to an industry leader for change, Anderson became one of our greatest inspirations by confirming that the axioms we believed in worked well in the important arena of business.

To people across the country, Ray Anderson is more than just the CEO of one of the largest carpet manufacturing companies in the world; he is a sustainability hero. Named TIME Magazine's

Greenest CEO of 2007, Anderson is a case study of how one leader's 'spear in the chest' moment changed an entire industry. It occurred in 1994 when he read Paul Hawken's book *The Ecology of Commerce*. Expecting no more than token fodder to address some environmental concerns from his employees, Anderson had the life changing realization that he was running one of the most wasteful, polluting, fossil fuel dependent companies in the world.

He was facing a 'wicked' challenge since his operation included a complex network of machine and yarn providers, vendors, waste managers, machine operators, mechanics and factories all over the world. Path dependency ran deep because the manufacturing processes to create carpet, including suppliers and vendors, were deeply entrenched in decades-old technology. His entire workforce was trained for these technologies, making their entrenchment self-reinforcing, much like the QWERTY keyboard.

Anderson's response was like seeing our axioms applied at a multi-national business level. He created a clear top-level vision to steer his one billion dollar a year company toward zero pollution and zero net energy use by 2020. This goal was truly transformative and would inspire and require great innovation. He assembled the Eco Dream Team, a diverse and interdisciplinary array of change agents that included progressive thinkers and designers, as well as stakeholders from throughout his plants.

While Anderson describes what ensued in great detail in his book *Midcourse Correction*, we had a once-in-a-lifetime opportunity to see for ourselves first hand. Due to our efforts on campus, I was invited with two other HUB members, Tamara and Vance, to Interface Carpet's flagship factory in Georgia for a weekend retreat and tour. My excitement went beyond staying in a Frank Lloyd Wright designed mansion, being hosted at a spa, and experiencing winter for the first time in years. For a manufacturing engineer who had almost left my profession due to the irresponsible conduct of one company, the opportunity to intimately experience the inner workings of a company that was doing it right was the best reward I could think of for our efforts. I felt like Charlie with the golden ticket.

We learned that Anderson brought carpet tiles, the two-foot by two-foot square sections that fit together and are easily removed and replaced, into mainstream use. His designers created patterns that look great no matter how the squares are configured, streamlining installation and making it easy to remove and replace just one section. Since traditional carpet is one continuous piece, if a stain occurs the entire carpet must be removed. So carpet tile greatly reduced unnecessary carpet waste. He addressed the old-style broadloom carpet that still needed disposal by building a carpet-recycling center right in his factory. He also greatly reduced the need for toxic glue with interlocking fasteners that hold the tiles together. In the carpet making business entire industrial size spools of yarn are often wasted when a thread snaps. Interface innovated new spools where the operator could mend the thread in minutes right on the line.

Anderson's innovations not only affected his own company, but transformed all suppliers in the industry. He created incrementally increasing demand for recycled yarn, requiring more each year. In this way he recognized that slow, cumulative changes that move irreversibly toward the end goal make consistent progress. While it took yarn companies a few years to be able to produce the full spectrum of color and texture, they were eventually able to do so and increase their own profits by reducing their use of virgin materials.

Anderson also understood the importance of the triple bottom line by ensuring his employees were fulfilled in their roles and responsibilities. Interface uses a strengths finding program to help workers identify career paths that would feel uniquely rewarding to each person in the company. Every employee no matter their position or rank is trained in the company's core values of sustainability. When we chatted with workers as we walked the factory floor, all understood sustainability and seemed proud of their place in making it happen in their company. Beyond being mere technicians, or cogs in the corporate wheel, each knew how everyone's roles contributed to the bigger picture and was able to be creative and innovative on the job due to this understanding. As such, at Interface Carpet the implementers are also advocates.

Ray Anderson risked his single bottom line when he took an early stand to transform his company to a triple bottom line focus, making Interface accountable beyond his or most industries. Although this was all new to everyone at Interface and throughout the entire carpet manufacturing industry, they took a brave step and let the next step emerge along their path to transformation. Interface Carpet has since cut dependence on fossil fuels by 45%, and water and landfill use by as much as 80%, all while increasing revenues by 6 million dollars annually. Anderson is a role model for all corporate and business leaders demonstrating that the environment, people and the planet are not tradeoffs, but can all benefit with focus, innovation and ingenuity.

A retiree after thirty-four years at IBM, Bob Willard shows how Anderson's success is not a chance occurrence. In his book *The Sustainability Advantage: Seven Business Case Benefits of a Triple Bottom Line*, he shows how to help executives tune into WIIFM (What's in it for Me?) rather than just WIIFW (What's in it for the World?). He lists the many business benefits of striving for change using the triple bottom line, such as addressing the high cost of turnover and winning and retaining the best talent. Willard outlines case studies that show employee retention and productivity increase when companies use the triple bottom line. Other benefits include increased revenues due to increased employee productivity and increased market share. He shares studies such as a Mercer/Angus Reid poll that found that companies leading the way to implementing changes with the triple bottom line gained disproportionate advantage since a strong environmental rating was a consistent predictor of profitability (Willard, 2002, p. 139). He offers a step-by-step approach to building business case scenarios that benefit people and the planet by leveraging these business advantages to increase profits.

I had a surprising opportunity in Hawaii to experience a large multi-national company operating under such a business strategy through a chance occurrence that would end up transforming the energy future of UH, as well as my own personal future. It began when our weekly commute across the city to Honolulu Community College (HCC) to volunteer our time resulted in being in the right place at the right time when the college decided to hire an Energy Service Company (ESCO). I had always admired one of the ESCO business models called Performance Contracting. In Performance Contracting, an ESCO provides the expertise to find every energy saving and power generating opportunity, all without additional cost burden to an organization since the expected savings are used to offset the project capital investment over the term of the contract. The customer benefits from no up-front cost, and the ESCO takes away all risk by guaranteeing the savings over a typical contract term of ten or twenty years. If their recommendations don't result in savings, the ESCO eats the loss. As such, they have every incentive to provide training and long-term maintenance to maximize savings. The ability of this model to help make large, systemic change without the sacrifice of upfront cost had always intrigued me so I closely followed the progress of the UH College system as they carefully selected an ESCO.

One of the original companies in the industry, Johnson Controls Inc. (JCI), won the contract for Maui College as well as the four community colleges on Oahu, including HCC. When we learned that their engineering experts were going to perform a lighting audit at HCC during the off-school hours of 9pm to 2am, we asked if we could tag along to learn and help out. They were thrilled that we were interested. Twenty student volunteers and I showed up with coffee in hand and the engineers enthusiastically shared everything we could ever want to know about a building's lighting into the wee hours of the morning. I also learned that besides being great guys that enjoyed sharing the passion of their work, involving the students reflected the company's focus of providing an educational component as part of their contracts on school campuses.

I had often thought it a lost learning opportunity that so many interesting energy projects occur in campus buildings with no involvement from the students. In my experience, every person from art to architecture majors love playing with a light meter or temperature gun as they learn about the building they spend much of their day occupying. Building energy use is interesting stuff when brought to life in the right way.

As I chatted with the engineers and realized how much my philosophies on 'learning by doing' gelled with those of Johnson Controls Inc., I asked to stay involved as they moved through their energy audits. As I remained engaged with the team, JCI eventually created a consulting contract to formalize our working relationship. Over my years in grad school I had turned down about a dozen great job and contract offers, and more than a few with six figure salaries, since I felt they would take me back to where I had started: working to live, not living to work. The opportunity to liaison with the JCI Sustainability Education Manager and JCI engineers around the country to gather the latest expertise and training for the college system, all while working with JCI and the faculty to co-create internships and curricula involving real life projects was a dream come true. When I graduated with my Masters in Urban Planning in the summer of 2010, I began the next chapter of my consulting career as the Johnson Controls Hawaii Education Consultant.

While I had found the next step of my career in another large multi-national company, many students in my internship class were much more interested in turning their passion into a new small business. For the local green economy to grow and thrive there is the need, and endless opportunity, for innovative new start-ups to prosper and create new jobs. Author Scott Cooney figured this out early when, as an MBA student, he was forced to write what he knew for a last-minute cram job on a marketing assignment.

He wrote a business plan for an eco-friendly landscaping business since he had done some landscape work for a summer and knew environmental issues pretty well. With green business as an unknown concept, it was met with skepticism, until a few years later when he decided to put his plan into action. He started the business and in a short time it was a great success. To expand his ever-growing market share, he began a green business directory, which was met with even greater skepticism since it seemed there were no more than a handful of green businesses in the Salt Lake City area where he lived. Within two years the directory contained well over 300 businesses. He personally interviewed each business owner to make sure they qualified for the directory, and along the way learned the ins and outs of how to make a small green business succeed.

He eventually decided to help aspiring eco-entrepreneurs everywhere start their dream businesses in his book *Build a Green Small Business: Profitable Ways to Become an Ecopreneur*, published by McGraw-Hill. From a green carpet cleaning business to a green bed and breakfast, he shares diverse strategies for starting the right business for any area of interest or expertise. He also shows how economic downturns in history have been periods of great entrepreneurial activity since companies have trimmed payrolls and are looking to outsource a lot of work to outside contractors. Ecopreneurs can build a reputation and a client base by beginning with contract work. They can also find talented employees and partners since there are many great people unemployed. My favorite advice from his greenbusinessowner.com site is: "Don't forget that a green business is still a job. Run one that you'll enjoy, are good at, and that allows you a level of comfort in your day-to-day life."

CHAPTER 14

Big Change for a Preferred Future

While HUB's axioms had proven useful for diverse projects throughout UH and in many examples in business I wondered if could they could be helpful for addressing an even bigger 'wicked' challenge, one that I and many believe is the most complex and important problem to address for Hawaii's future prosperity and survival, especially in Hawaii: an independent energy future.

The world's current energy landscape encompasses many path dependent approaches that have combined to entrench our reliance on fossil fuel. Recall that path dependency explains how the set of decisions one faces for any given circumstance is limited by the decisions one has made in the past, or why the same path is chosen even in the face of better options. Self-reinforcing processes are one of the main reasons for this, and this is very true when it comes to entrenched fossil fuel dependence. For example, thirty years and three trillion US dollars have been invested to produce a typical car fleet (Kelly, Cashore, Bernstein, & Auld, 2009, p. 17). We see that there is great incentive for stakeholders to recoup their investments.

Yet on the other hand, while many say that the only two things we can be sure of are death and taxes, a third certainty can surely be added — the end of cheap oil.

About 90% of the world's energy consumption comes from fossil fuels, all of which are non-renewable resources. With this level of consumption, it is inevitable that the time will come when there is not enough fossil fuel available to run our economy. This deadline depends on two factors: the consumption rate and the amount of fossil fuel remaining. If consumption remains constant, early estimates showed us running out of oil in 2050. On the other extreme, if consumption continues at an exponential growth of 2%, the world could run out of oil around 2035, and an exponential consumption growth of 10% reduces that number to 2020 (McFarland, Hunt, & Campbell, 2001, p. 2-18).

To complicate matters, as supplies peak and then start to dwindle prices will most probably increase due to scarcity. This will cause a decrease in the consumption as oil becomes more and more expensive. Consumption will level off and then decline according to the 'peak oil' model introduced in the 1950s by Dr. M. King Hubbert (McFarland, Hunt, & Campbell, 2001). Regardless of when it hits, peak oil poses a considerable threat to most of the world, but will be exceptionally devastating for Hawaii, which imports even our most basic necessities (Dator, The Unholy Trinity, Plus One, 2009, p. 2). The two legs of Hawaii's economy, tourism and the military, both heavily rely on cheap transport fuel and over 95% of our electricity is created from burning imported fossil fuel (Electric, 2008). Life in Hawaii as we know it will literally grind to a halt as oil becomes unaffordable and inaccessible.

Like most of the world, Hawaii would benefit from efficiently adapting to a new model of energy supply regardless of when the peak might occur (Graefe, 2009, p. 12). Ultimately, Hawaii has no choice but to become energy independent. How current oil supplies are used and what type of technology is created and implemented will determine whether Hawaii's energy future will be one of abundant or scarce energy resources. Conservation and efficiency measures would minimize energy needs and the remaining demand would be met by renewable sources. In this way, Hawaii would become energy self-sufficient and we could export this knowledge in the form of services and eco-tourism. If the decision makers in Hawaii were to plan appropriately, Dator describes the following preferred future:

> Beaches will be open, surfing spots — and the roads to and from them — uncrowded, mass tourism no longer our primary industry, mom and pop stores will sell locally-made and produced foods and goods, neighbors will get to know one another again, and we will no longer need to lock our doors. Best of all, the most life enhancing of traditional Hawaiian values and ways of life might come to be the norm for all of us here (Dator, The Unholy Trinity, Plus One, 2009, p.42).

This vision of a transformative preferred future may seem like a far off utopian dream, yet all the resources, technology and policies exist today to make this a reality.

Renewable energy (RE) in its many forms is more abundant in Hawaii than in most places on Earth. It is entirely within Hawaii's reach to produce enough renewable energy to power our islands and we have every motivation to do so. Since Hawaii depends on imported fossil fuel for over 95% of its energy needs, it is especially vulnerable to potential disruptions and price spikes from international political turbulence and shortages due to peak oil. Hawaii's extreme vulnerability due to oil dependence creates the incentive and opportunity to explore renewable energy. So if it is more possible here than in most places on Earth and we have a magnified incentive to do so, why isn't Hawaii energy independent?

I first looked to the stakeholders and found there was indeed a long-standing polarization in Hawaii between the renewable energy industry, along with their supporting community activist groups, and the public electricity utility, Hawaii Electric Co. (HECO). We had learned that seeing others as human and finding common ground could diffuse opposing viewpoints. What could be the common ground between the utility and the RE sector?

I learned that electricity sales had flatlined, meaning stayed constant, in Hawaii for years. HECO was actively looking for a way to ensure their profits didn't decrease; they were open to new possibilities. Could RE generation be the common ground for Hawaii's energy stakeholders?

When I began exploring this question in 2008, one of the only top-level guidelines for energy production, the Renewable Portfolio Standard (RPS), mandated that 10% of the total power produced came from the state's renewable energy production. HECO had reported 18% RE production, which would make it seem that Hawaii had exceeded its goals. While this is true on paper, a deeper look into these numbers revealed that only about 5% came from natural renewable energy sources. So where did the remaining 13% of reported renewable energy come from? The answer is waste and conservation, which Hawaii counts as renewable energy.

Oahu burns about 50% of our waste, which created 4% of Hawaii's total energy in 2008 (Electric, 2008, p.5). Conservation measures through the utility's conservation program called Demand Side Management (DSM) counted for the remaining 9% (Electric, 2008, p. 5). While our numbers looked good, in reality we were not making a true effort toward capitalizing on our natural renewable energy sources. So how could we set realistic, measurable goals that would move us toward true renewable energy generation?

Sustainable UH had used professional standards, best practices, and successful case studies to find realistic goals. Applying this axiom to Hawaii's energy policy began with an investigation into the RPS criteria for other states. We learned that solar and wind or other defined technologies are the only allowable sources of energy to count toward the RPS in many states. Hawaii's permissive criteria, coupled with its low 10% requirement, made it one of the least aggressive states in renewable energy policy when compared to national benchmarks and best practices. With this RPS as the goal for RE in the state, the hope for RE as a common ground seemed bleak until a statewide initiative was launched showing again how change starts with clear direction from top-level leadership.

In 2008 the State's leaders including the Governor, utility, and other state agencies, surprised all stakeholders by introducing the most aggressive energy policy in the country. Called the Hawaii Clean Energy Initiative (HCEI), it set the goal of reducing Hawaii's dependence on fossil fuel by 70% by 2030. This certainly represented an end target beyond business as usual and was an overarching goal that would inspire change.

Much as the Chancellor's Energy Policy goals on campus had fostered bridges of support from the utility and state agencies, the HCEI drew support from national agencies such as the Department of Energy (DOE), the Environmental Protection Agency (EPA), and the National Renewable Energy Laboratory (NREL). And much as the grassroots and upper-level communities on campus were bridged since their goals were in alignment, there was rarely a conversation amongst energy stakeholders from HECO to small RE companies in Hawaii over the next few years that wasn't in some direct or indirect way linked to the HCEI.

14.1 PROGRESSIVE INCREMENTS FOR CUMULATIVE CHANGE

For the HCEI to be successful, 30% of the 70% energy reduction was to come from conservation. This seemed very realistic to us since our energy assessments at Sustainable Saunders and throughout the state showed that most homes and buildings could easily eliminate 20-50% of their energy bills through conservation and efficiency. We also learned there is a difference. Conservation refers to switching things off, while efficiency refers to accomplishing the same outcome by using less electricity. For example, turning lights off is conservation. Replacing traditional incandescent bulbs with compact fluorescent lights (CFLs) that use 75% less energy to produce the same amount of light is efficiency. Removing your basement refrigerator is conservation. Replacing it with a small bar fridge (since you only keep a case of beer in there anyway) is efficiency.

Again, it must be emphasized that conservation is not about sacrifice, which has been the unfortunate perception for decades. Despite his advocacy for doing right by the planet, Jimmy Carter did the world a great disservice in the early 1970s by appearing on television sitting in a dim room huddled in a sweater encouraging Americans to conserve energy. This portrayal of discomfort linked conservation to sacrifice, and many of our efforts on campus strove to reposition sustainability as increased happiness and prosperity. We actually *increased* comfort and health conditions for occupants when we cut the energy bill by $150,000 annually. For the HCEI to be successful, it would have to promote and find incentives for efficiency and conservation that increased the triple bottom line for residents and business owners in Hawaii.

The state was already ahead of the game by providing tax rebates for the number one efficiency technology for Hawaii's homes: solar thermal hot water heating.

Solar thermal panels placed on a roof use the heat of the sun to warm water before it passes through an electric water heater, and require about 90% less electricity to create the same enjoyable hot shower. DBEDT has found that in most non-air-conditioned homes in Hawaii water heating represents about 30-50% of the utility bill. Solar technology can therefore reduce a home's energy bill by 27-45%. When combined with state tax credits, it pays for itself in less than two years and the subsequent savings for decades go right into the homeowner's pocket. It's no wonder about a quarter of Hawaii's homes heat their water by the sun. Considered the best bang for your efficiency buck, Hawaii recently passed a law mandating that all new buildings must have solar hot water heating.

There are other small no-cost changes that would put money back into every home and business in Hawaii. For example, few people realize that plugged in appliances still consume costly electricity even when they are turned off. Cell phone chargers, printers, stereos, kitchen appliances, computers and many appliances that use electricity draw some power, called phantom loads or phantom power, when plugged in yet not in use. In fact, the U.S. Department of Energy determined that 75% of the electricity used by most home electronics and appliances is actually phantom power (Energy, 2010). Since appliances account for 20% of most home bills, most homes and businesses could reduce their overall energy bill by 15% by simply plugging in their chargers and appliances only when needed.

Rather than running around your house unplugging cords all day, you could plug electronic devices into a power strip and with one flick of a switch, shut down the whole strip, cutting off phantom power. Occupancy-sensing power strips do this automatically when they detect that a room is empty, and some come with timers. Smart strips have one control plug that senses a drop in electricity use and turns off all other items plugged into the strip. For example, you could plug your computer into the control socket and when you turn your computer off, your printer, desk lamp and any other items plugged into the strip would also switch off.

There are also more widespread incremental measures that could pay for themselves in months and could greatly impact the electricity consumption of Hawaii's businesses, agencies and institutions. For example, BC Hydro, the largest electric utility in British Columbia, Canada, serves 1.8 million customers and has extensive expertise in the field of electricity generation and conservation. In August 2009, the BC Hydro Power Authority, which operates BC Hydro, applied Faronics Power Save to all of its laptops and desktop computers nearly simultaneously and instantly from its central console. The software analyzes CPU application activity, disk, keyboard, and mouse status and then automatically reduces computer energy use by placing it in standby mode after a determined length of inactivity, such as fifteen or thirty minutes.

Although BC Hydro's computers and LCD monitors are some of the most efficient available since they are Energy-Star-compliant (which can be 50% more energy efficient than standard computers) and have installed standby modes, they still experienced substantial savings after adding Faronics Power Save (North, 2010, p. 3). A typical computer in standby consumes about 3W of energy, compared with 85W to 127W when it is fully active (North, 2010, p. 3). Power Save also cuts power used by the computer's peripherals such as the hard drive and monitor. The study found that for about 8,000 (as of early December 2009) PCs equipped with Power Save at BC Hydro, approximately 1 million kilowatt hours (kWh) have been saved annually (North, 2010, p. 4). License costs plus maintenance amounted to $110,600 over a three-year period and the pilot, planning, and implementation labor cost was approximately $35,000, for a total cost of $145,600 (North, 2010, p. 4).

At $0.26 per kWh for electricity in Hawaii the total three-year savings would be $780,000. The return on investment (ROI), the point at which the cost would be paid back through the savings, would occur in less than seven months. The University of Hawaii's IT department reports 55,000 computers in the system. At the lower campus cost of electricity of $0.22 per kWh, an extrapolation of the findings from BC Hydro estimates that $1,499,752 could be saved annually. Once implemented, this software is irreversible and would continue to provide long-term benefits, making it a truly cumulative increment toward Hawaii's transformative goals.

14.2 Identifying and Leveraging Triple Bottom Line Benefits

Within these irreversible, incremental changes, Hawaii has many existing projects that act as pilots in that they provide proof of concept with triple bottom line benefits.

The use of natural daylight is one example. A study of Department of Education (DOE) schools by a local architecture firm, Ferrero Choi, found that the single most important strategy in achieving the economic benefits that result in operation savings is day lighting (Choi, 2007). Many studies have also shown that human performance improves with natural light. One study of all second through fifth grade students in three large and climatically different school districts found that those in classrooms with the most window area or day lighting scored 7 to 18% higher on standardized tests than those with the least window area or day lighting (Heschong, 2002, p. 66). While there may be concern that sunlight will cause an additional strain on the air conditioning, window tinting is an affordable and non-intrusive way to ensure heat does not accompany the light that enters the room. Day lighting offers huge opportunity for triple bottom line benefits.

14.3 Mobilizing Community Level Action to Implement Systemic Change

Our axioms tell us that in implementing systemic change, grassroot efforts must be engaged to achieve top-level priorities. In the energy landscape of Hawaii, every person and organization with an electricity bill needs to be empowered if Hawaii is to reach its goals.

The first order of business in enabling community, bottom-up action would be to democratize the grid. Power is presently disseminated in one direction, from the utility to each and every home and business in Hawaii. We have become so accustomed to being mere recipients of power, that the idea of being able to create it ourselves, with perhaps enough excess to share and sell to others, represents a transformative paradigm shift. This new paradigm is called 'distributed generation'.

In the distributed generation paradigm, energy comes from distributed sources including homes, businesses, and wind farms rather than just centrally controlled power plants. The grid acts as a dispatcher that receives electricity generated from this huge number of sources and distributes it where needed. The grid becomes a two-way street and can sense how much energy each building has provided so they can be paid accordingly. It also determines where the energy needs to go and delivers it in the most efficient manor. This is called a smart grid for obvious reasons, and, when perfected, it can act like your own personal day trader, selling electricity to optimize your profits when electricity is priced high during peak demand, and buying when it is priced low due to little demand. It can also communicate with smart meters that allow you to monitor your home and even your appliances real time via the web. Smart meters are already being rolled out with over 5 million installed through PG&E's service area in California. Responding to email and phone notifications of energy use in real time, over 70% of customers have reduced their energy bills due to real time feedback.

The next iteration of technology development allows smart meters to not only monitor, but also control appliances. For example, if you have excess solar energy from your roof and communication with the grid determines that it's not a profitable time to sell, the smart meter turns on your washing machine instead and uses the energy at the lowest cost to you. Perhaps you set the washing machine to run sometime in the next 12 hours at the most optimum time as determined by your smart meter. With you in the driver's seat controlling the parameters, the smart grid and meters work together to efficiently use electricity while saving and making you money.

The smart grid can be thought of as a means of democratizing energy use since customers are able to have a voice and choice in how their power is created. The smart grid also creates a market for customers to be producers as well as consumers. It allows grid participants to monitor their energy use so they can change their behavior to lower their electricity bill, which impacts the entire energy landscape of a region beyond mere savings for individual users. For example, in Hawaii peak power use is from 4:00 to 7:00 pm, when residents come home at the end of the workday and turn on their high-powered appliances.

HECO reports that the island of Oahu uses about 1260 mega watts (MW) of electricity during this time. Of course the utility must have enough power plants to meet this peak demand (Electric, 2008). Since outside of these hours only a portion of this energy is needed, many of our power plants are in existence simply to meet these peak afternoon needs. Put more simply, if we were to change our behavior to conserve energy, use efficient technology or use smart meters to reduce the electricity we use from 4:00 to 7:00 pm, called 'peak shaving', we could instantly close down some of the fossil fuel-burning power plants on Oahu.

If a smart grid was able to receive renewable energy from every residential and commercial building in Hawaii, how could typical individuals and businesses participate in this new energy landscape? The grid would enable them to turn their home or business into a renewable energy producer rather than energy consumer and transform their energy bill into an energy paycheck.

The upfront cost of renewable energy is usually the biggest perceived barrier to this path, and yet there are many ways to get around this. Starting with two states in January 2009 and growing to 16 states one year later, a program called Property Assessed Clean Energy (PACE) is solving the problem of upfront solar and energy efficiency retrofits across the country. Homeowners can take advantage of a city loan for these items, and then pay it back through property tax bills over the next 15 to 20 years (Pace, 2010). If you were told you needed to pay $28,000 (a typical cost for a home's solar array) to use your cell phone for the next 20 years, even the most talkative consumer might recoil, yet paying $119 a month for 20 years adds up to just that. PACE removes the shock of the upfront cost and creates a manageable monthly payment for renewables and energy efficiency measures. This doesn't reduce the equity in your home, and the solar power system and any tax liability both transfer if you sell your home. With this policy in place in Hawaii, home owners would no longer have a financial barrier, and all homes would be able to pay a fraction of their energy bill, pocket the remaining savings, and collectively move Hawaii toward being a fossil fuel-free state.

14.4 Addressing Path Dependency to Implement New Technologies

There are many technologies that would significantly contribute to Hawaii's transformative energy future. Most would likely conflict with the path dependency of oil. In order to overcome this path dependency, pilots would have to be performed with widespread citizen participation.

Consider the case of electric vehicles. Besides providing energy use information that may prompt residents to use less energy during peak hours, the smart grid can help reduce peak load in another way. Electric cars that are charged during the evening off-peak hours may be Hawaii's fastest ticket to peak shaving. A New Zealand vehicle-to-home study modeled a single house that charged a single electric vehicle. The car did a daily round trip commute of 30 miles and when it returned home, the high-powered appliances were run from the remaining charge on its battery. The study assumed that the car was at work from 9am to 5pm and that the battery experienced a constant power drain while at work. The commute consumed 25% of the battery, and had ample charge left when it returned home to power high-power appliances, while base appliances that constantly drew lower levels of electricity continued to run from the grid (Hines, 2009, p. 1).

The study also determined that the commute could consume up to 70% of the battery charge and still successfully run the appliances (Hines, 2009, p. 3). This scenario reduced the peak power demand of the household by 70% from 10kW to 3kW (Hines, 2009, p. 4). By utilizing the remaining energy in the car battery in the evening during peak power demand, households could shave Hawaii's peak load, effectively reducing our need for some of our power plants without making a single other change.

Electric Vehicles are just one example of a technology or process that would require widespread implementation. And again the axioms prove useful considering that it would be ideal to deploy a pilot program in Hawaii, if even for a short time. Once residents realized how short commute distances are in Hawaii and how much money they could save, there would be the opportunity for widespread acceptance.

14.5 Mobilizing Change Agents

Effective change agents are those that have demonstrated passion and positive action even when the path is not easy. This can certainly be said of the many RE, conservation, and efficiency companies in Hawaii who have been working hard for decades to diversify and transform Hawaii's energy landscape. They are early adopters, passionate about their technologies and solutions. They are also diverse, ranging from sun and wind to efficiency and conservation. For their passion, drive, and diversity, they should be identified by the state as effective change agents that Hawaii would do well to leverage. But how?

We certainly learned that change agents are effective when they enjoy optimal experiences. Since optimal experience embodies joy, creativity and knowledge matching the challenge, then the ability to successfully grow their businesses would create optimal experience for RE, conservation, and efficiency companies, making them productive agents for the HCEI goals. The state could leverage these companies in many ways.

We could first strive to 'free the grid' as previously discussed, allowing an open free market for unfettered growth of renewable energy generation. Grid security and the assurance of uninterrupted power generation remain a paramount concern of the utility, which advocates maintaining planning control to ensure power quality and consistency. This tension between a free open electrical market and a regulated market is central to many current and proposed policies in the HCEI.

Ideally the HCEI would promote no system-wide caps on the amount of renewable energy allowed on the grid on any island, yet at the time of writing there is a limit on each circuit of no more than 15% of peak circuit demand (Initiative, 2008, p. 28). This limit effectively functions as a cap and does not foster the large-scale renewable energy generation that could make Hawaii energy independent. Accomplishing the HCEI's goal of replacing 40% of the State's current electricity generation with RE will be impossible unless the 15% circuit capacity is eventually lifted or completely eliminated.

Obligating utilities to purchase renewable energy is the most desirable regulation for stimulating investment in the rapid, large-scale renewable generation needed to move Hawaii towards its aggressive goals, as has been done in the country leading the world in solar installations: Germany (Solarbuzz, 2010). Germany's success is attributed to its Feed in Tariff (FIT), which obliges utilities to purchase energy and feed it into the grid at a guaranteed price for a guaranteed amount of time (Wustenhagen, 2004, p. 1685). This sends a strong, clear market signal stimulating investment in small and large-scale renewable energy generation beyond self-use. It also reduces barriers such as cost and time associated with negotiating interconnection on a case-by-case basis removing barriers and attracting investment.

"FITs similar to the German model have proven to be the most successful mechanism for stimulating investment in renewable electricity generation worldwide" (Wustenhagen, 2004, p. 1685). "FITs have resulted in more installed generating capacity, as well as more robust competition among manufacturers, and have stimulated more renewable technology development than any other policy mechanism. Only a model based on guaranteed FITs enables a quick and broad implementation of renewable energy" (Wustenhagen, 2004, p. 1691).

All FITs are not created equal, and the final parameters for Hawaii's FIT, which are still being worked out at the time of writing, will determine if this policy masks business as usual or truly provides the clear market signal Hawaii needs to accomplish its goals. A properly designed FIT mandates paying a **premium** price for electricity generation for a time window long enough for large-scale financers to recoup their investments, such as for twenty years. If there are caps on the amount of electricity to be purchased, then the model is more like a request for proposal (RFP) process where companies bid for limited market share rather than participate in an open, business-friendly market. Properly designed, an **uncapped** FIT that pays a long-term premium would move control of energy development from the regulated utility into a transparent market leading to rapid, wide-scale renewable energy, ultimately accomplishing the state's HCEI goals while growing a strong, local industry around renewable energy.

AND SO IT CONTINUES ...

In writing our story, I hope that this model that emerged from our efforts and built a nationally recognized movement for change throughout our campus and state will also prove useful for you. The path to change is challenging by any measure, but for those involved in the Sustainable UH story it has provided great growth, deep fulfillment, and a lot of good times as well. From our 'Board Meetings' that involved strategic planning while surfing together, to being invited to incredible conferences to share our story, to advocating for policy that would allow our lessons to replicate, to dancing all night to celebrate our milestones, we were stoked on all the ways we move toward change. We held our meetings ocean-side, or over a potluck at each other's homes, traveled together to conferences, played soccer, went on hikes to inspire new ideas, and in many ways merged our live-work-play lives into one big community.

When I think of the sadness I experienced in those moments when I felt like a cog in a machine as the many aspects of my life were segregated from each other, I realize now that I live the exact opposite life. My work comes from my passion, my teammates have become friends, and we work hard and play hard together. I have come to realize that we have created the modern-day version of what existed before the industrial revolution — integrated lives.

As a lecturer in the Honor's program at the University of Hawaii, a PhD student in Political Science, a researcher for DBEDT and Hawaii's Workforce Development Council, the President of the Sustainability Association of Hawaii, and the Hawaii Educational Consultant for Johnson Controls, I have created a meaningful, well-paying, sustainable career doing everything I'm passionate about. Daily I feel the rewards of a lifestyle where work and play feel the same, and where the path of change feels like an exciting adventure — an open landscape of possibilities and endless collaborations. Years ago I never would have thought it possible, but now I feel equally stoked if I wake up and have ten meetings lined up or if I have a leisurely day at the beach planned instead. And one of the most rewarding parts of this path is that my students keep becoming my colleagues as they are also hired into meaningful careers making change aligned with their passions. Whether in Sustainable UH or graduated into Hawaii's green workforce, we remain an entrepreneurial team of pioneers.

Even though working toward change brings up every resistance imaginable, and takes everything in us to overcome the challenges, it's ultimately an exciting and rewarding existence. Whether working on small changes in daily life, or on bigger systemic changes, we hope you too may have found something in our journey that perhaps makes the process fun and fulfilling, and inspires you most of all to keep going!

Evolving Sustainability as the Vehicle for Change

S ustainability is the word most associated with the type of change discussed in this book, and as such it deserves some discussion. Sustainability has served a wonderful purpose since sweeping the planet as perhaps the first global movement of its kind. Paul Hawken (2007) writes about it in his aptly titled *Blessed Unrest: How the Largest Movement in the World Came into Being and Why No One Saw it Coming*. The concept has been used to transform corporations into community stewards, win politicians' elections and secure grants for grassroots organizations. Yet groups have spent years agonizing over its very definition and struggling to identify how to incorporate it. There is so much emphasis on achieving sustainability, yet most don't know where to begin.

From the worldview that participants in society create reality through shared ideological constructs, sustainability is meant to act as a valuable identity-shaping concept through guidelines for collective and individual decision-making. Yet those who have adopted this overarching construct, especially planners, struggle to accurately define or operationalize sustainability. It is characterized as a 'fuzzy' concept, which is defined as possessing two or more alternative meanings, rendering it impossible to define and apply reliably (Gunder, 2006, p. 211).

'Sustainable Development Master Plans' have been criticized for being wish lists of goals and impractical implementation steps because of the overall vagueness of sustainability (Campbell, 1996, p. 14). For example, a 2000 study outlined six principles that characterize the concept of sustainable development and used them to evaluate 30 comprehensive community and urban plans to determine how well their policies support sustainable development. The study found no significant differences in the extent of sustainability principles implemented between the plans that stated an intention to integrate sustainable development and those that did not (Berke & Conroy, 2000, p. 21). Why have sustainability and sustainable development often not delivered on their ideals?

An exploration of the current limitations of sustainability begins with the question: shouldn't we be trying to do more than simply sustain? To *sustain* is to "prolong, lengthen or extend"[1] something already in existence. It also means to "suffer, undergo or carry the weight of."[2] Painting the future as a struggle to simply extrapolate the known leaves absolutely no room for hope, inspiration, and creativity, or for the emergence of something … new! Perhaps we could expand our understanding of sustainability with some other more inspiring words.

Futurist Jan Huston uses the word 'evolvability' to describe what society could be striving for (Huston, 1998, p. 436). Evolvability is based on the words *evolve*, which is to "develop, to gain through experience"[3] and *evolution*, which is "a process in which something passes by degrees to a different stage (especially a more advanced or mature stage) often leading to new traits"[4]. In her book *Thrivability*, Jean Russell introduces my favorite term to describe the prosperous transformation that society could be inspired by. *Thrivability* is based on the word *thrive*, which means "to prosper."

Other common words also help expand the perception of

sustainability. *Emergence* is "to come into view, as from concealment or obscurity."[5] A *transformation* is "a marked change, as in appearance or character, usually for the better."[6] *Evolvability, thrivability, emergence* and *transformation* all foster hope and vision, yet we have instead made the word *sustainability* our guiding principle, suggesting that the best we can do is sacrifice and toil to attempt to continue life as we know it.

Sustainability, as it is currently understood, suggests we cannot or should not hope for anything different, anything more. How did it come to be that sustainability is viewed as simple survival? An emerging issues analysis based on theory from the academic field of Futures Studies shows how sustainability has been co-opted throughout its history.

SUSTAINABILITY EMERGES DURING A GLOBAL PARADIGM OF SCARCITY

Why does the term sustainability as we know it exist today? A Futures Studies methodology called 'emerging issues analysis' explores such questions by asking when did it emerge, who brought it into existence, and for what purpose? The theory that supports this analysis shows that for all existing issues that are well known in society, there is an 'S' curve that describes the path of their emergence plotted over time (Dator, *From Tsunamis to Long Waves and Back*, 1999, p. 4). At one point the issue was unknown and barely perceptible in society, and then eventually became known at a rapidly-accelerating rate, until the top of the 'S' flattens out since the issue has saturated society. By studying the social, political, and economic factors affecting each of these regions of the curve, much can be revealed about the meaning that accompanied the issue's emergence and acceptance.

Charting the appearance of the terms 'sustainability' and 'sustainable development' in the Cambridge Scientific Abstracts database over the decades since their first appearance, a clear 'S' curve appears in Figure 7:

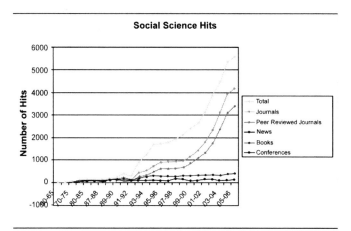

Figure 7: Presence of "Sustainability" and "Sustainable Development" in Scientific Abstract Titles Over Time (Created by the author)

In the early 1970s the word 'sustainability' began to show up in academic journals as shown in Figure 7. This coincides with a United Nations Conference in Sweden in 1972 where sustainability was first defined as:

* the interdependence of human beings and the natural environment;

* the links between economic development, social development, and environmental protection;

* the need for a global vision and common principles (Nations, 1972).

A search for other significant publications in that year reveals that early in 1972 The Club of Rome issued their first report, 'The Limits to Growth' with worldwide impact. The report stressed for the first time in history the importance of the environment, and the essential links with population and energy (Rome, 1972). The word sustainability came into being at the same time as global scarcity and limits were introduced. Since 'the need for a global vision and common principles' was identified as a time of a perception of lack, sustainability in terms of simply surviving became the focus, rather than being viewed as evolving, thriving, emerging, and transforming, as might have happened in more prosperous times.

SUSTAINABILITY IS CO-OPTED AS SUSTAINABLE DEVELOPMENT

In 1987 the word sustainability gained a noticeable increase in use at the same time as the World Commission on Environment and Development (Brundtland Commission, 1987). This conference first defined sustainable development as follows:

> Development that meets the needs of the present without compromising the ability of future generations to meet their own needs ... sustainable development is a process of change in which exploitation of resources, the direction of investments, the orientation of technological development, and institutional change are all in harmony and enhance both current and future potential to meet human needs and aspirations. (Development, 1987, p. 43).

This definition has been widely criticized since sustainable development alone does not lead to sustainability and may in fact support the longevity of the unsustainable path (Yanarella & Levine, 1992). This definition prioritized the sustainability of economic development for both present and future generations, and proposed that the environment be preserved so that it could be exploited for development, both now and in the future. Another problem with this definition is that, practically stated, it doesn't provide useful guidance for planning and decision-making. Both definition of 'needs' and how to meet needs are subjective, thus it lacks the substantive guidance that could assist with real life decision-making. Despite the criticism for disguising business as usual, its limited practical usefulness, and the fact that it is actually a definition for development, this remains the most commonly sited definition of sustainability.

Returning to the 'S' curve chart (Fig. 7), an even more noticeable jump in the use of the word sustainability occurred in 1992 at the time of the United Nations Conference on Environment and Development, also known as the Earth Summit. This was a major conference held in Rio de Janeiro in 1992. The title of the conference, as well as the title of the main resulting document, the "Rio Declaration on Environment and Development" emphasized the 'right to development followed by the duty of sustainable development' (Nations, Report of the United Nations Conference on the Human Environment, 1972). With this definition, again sustainability became a subset of development rather than a stand-alone overarching goal, and development was reinforced as the ultimate goal.

SUSTAINABILITY POSITIONS THE ECONOMY AND SOCIETY AGAINST THE ENVIRONMENT

The original 1972 Brundtland definition created a discourse that set economic and societal concerns in opposition of the environment. This definition of sustainability emphasized the links between "economic development, social development, and environmental protection", but also provides insight into how these three elements are often viewed as tradeoffs. This wording actually positioned them in opposition since the "economic" and "social" aspects were related to "development," while the "environment" was deemed as needing "protection." The environment is described as weak and requiring something of us. It positions environmental elements, including natural resources deemed as commodities, as needing a champion to defend them from economic and social development, essentially placing the environment as mutually exclusive from the economy and society and operating under opposing forces. This remains a challenge in the concept of sustainability today where the environment, society and the economy are seen as opposing entities that require tradeoffs rather than as mutually enhancing and simultaneously beneficial.

Evidence of this discourse is found everywhere today. For example, Hawaii's 2050 Task Force on Sustainability released its draft report containing the following graph summarizing its state-wide poll results:

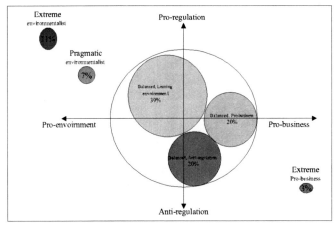

Figure 8: Hawaii's 2050 Task Force on Sustainability Survey Results (2050, 2008)

The x-axis in Figure 8 clearly depicts the environment and business (the economy) as opposites. While sustainability is popularly claimed to be a balance and interconnection of society, economy and environment, when put to practice, the environment is often pegged against the others.

Making Sustainability Useful in Real-Life Planning

These early definitions of sustainability that have permeated discussions for decades have one, assumed a paradigm of scarcity; two, charted a course that settles for sustaining rather than striving for evolving, thriving, emerging, and transforming; three, co-opted the term for sustainable development that propagates the status quo goal of economic growth; and four, positioned the economy and society against the environment rather than promoting the synergy of the three.

So while the initiative that was to be our vehicle for change was named Sustainable Saunders, we didn't have a definition of sustainability that could guide us. We had watched too many organizations spend so much time trying to define it that they had prolonged the process of implementing it. We knew the word sustainability would still have to be used as an overarching goal, but we needing something more substantial to guide us. We needed to make it practical and useful for real life planning. So rather than a definition, our team assembled a set of guiding principles that we would rely on to create goals, design processes, measure our success, and maybe most importantly provide a common language.

Sustainability as
Seven Guiding Principles

As new cohorts of students joined the HUB, we found that while we had basic understanding of many of the same concepts, we used different words to describe the same thing. We were spending valuable time together translating to get everyone on the same page. Inevitably, a HUB member would bring a new idea, or require someone to explain a concept we used daily, and we needed a more efficient means of communication. Our solution came in the best way it can in academia; it was time to create curriculum. We needed an entry point to the information that would be accessible and interesting to any level of experience or interest and that would provide the common language and quick decision criteria our team needed. In a HUB brainstorming session, we named the course "Sustainability 101, Basic Training for Sustainable Action." During a system-wide faculty workshop with representatives from all ten campuses in the UH system, I shared the concept and received a great reaction. We were apparently onto something.

Krista Hiser, a tenured professor specializing in sustainability, encouraged me to develop the curriculum with the goal that I would train two people from each campus to simultaneously teach the course on Earth Day, 2008. For the first time, the same course would be taught on all ten campuses in Hawaii simultaneously!

With such a worthy goal, I was inspired, but had no idea how to develop curriculum.

Much as I have encouraged HUB members facing a huge new task, I took a stab at making a draft that at least made sense to me. I then partnered with Krista Hiser to hone it into real curriculum. She introduced the idea of taking the concepts and developing modules so the course could be taught in one fell swoop, or the modules could be spread out and/or integrated into existing curriculum. I ensured each would take less than fifteen minutes to teach, included case studies from UH and Hawaii, as well as tied into national and global trends. I also started with the simplest concepts, and layered the language learned in early modules into later modules, building context for the student. Rather than a hefty document, I designed the course as a power point presentation with the main points included as bullet points in the note section of each slide. In this way it was easy to 'train the trainer,' and the simultaneous ten-campus Earth Day event was a success!

Krista had further ideas for sharing the curriculum. We developed an on-line version at Kapi'olani Community College designed for small businesses in Hawaii. I narrated each module for students to download. Each contained local business case studies, and at the end of each module we posed a question to be discussed on-line with the class. We then recorded pod casts and short video clips of examples in Hawaii that students could download to accompany each module. We also added a ten question on-line quiz that referenced the material in each module, as well as the accompanying media.

Since these early iterations of the course, I have found these modules to be widely received by many diverse audiences. When I began teaching a capstone class, I taught it to my students, as well as new HUB members every semester so they were immediately up to speed and able to communicate and work with experienced HUB members, as well as leaders and experts in business, government and the community. I also taught the course as a three-hour workshop through Outreach College at UHM, which is a non-credit branch of the university. People from businesses, non-profits, public and private schools, government agencies, the electrical and water utilities and many other diverse groups have attended over the years, sometimes coming back repeatedly. It always amazes me how those ranging from little experience to experts all gain from the material, as well as the opportunity to workshop real challenges with each other.

I have also been continually pleased with how versatile the modules are for varied areas of focus. For example, I worked with one of the original HUB members, Vance Arakaki, who has extensive background in his family's construction business, to tailor the curriculum for the Honolulu Community College (HCC) Construction Academy. We trained twenty-two high school construction teachers as well as faculty at HCC who then incorporated the modules into their existing classes. Integrating the fifteen-minute modules was manageable and did not require curriculum review, so within a semester all high school and higher education construction streams could be learning the seven guiding principles (see next page).

Krista and I share a vision of engaging faculty to incorporate these modules into all streams of academia, creating Sustainability Across the Curriculum (SAC). SAC is modeled after the Writing Across the Curriculum (WAC) movement that swept through higher education across the country. WAC incorporates writing into all disciplines, rather than requiring only students in writing-focused degrees to be proficient in writing. In the same spirit, the idea is that no matter what path a student might take through higher education, they would graduate understanding the seven guiding principles. They wouldn't necessarily associate them with sustainability; they would rather associate them as useful rules of thumb in the context of their own discipline. While this has just begun by tailoring modules for small business, construction, and graphic design, the versatility is already proven and the potential for integration of these concepts throughout higher education is an exciting, and very possible, preferred future to strive for.

The seven core principles are briefly described as follows:

PRINCIPLE 1: THE TRIPLE BOTTOM LINE

This principle is thoroughly outlined in Chapter 13 of this book. Rather than considering people, planet and profits as trade-offs, it is the simultaneous benefit of the three.

PRINCIPLE 2: CLOSED LOOP CYCLES

Since all of nature operates efficiently in interconnected cycles, Principle 2 proposes that we should strive for cyclic, not linear, human processes such as turning waste into food or fuel. The HUB also applies this philosophy to human interactions. If you look at negativity and conflict as pollution, the goal is to turn it into compost for common ground. For example, you know someone got linear when you walk away feeling drained, so learn how to make interactions cyclic where you both walk away feeling energized. Hence this module introduces the language of "close the loop" and "make it cyclic." Global examples include eco-industrial parks for circular economies in China. Re-Use Hawaii is a non-profit that takes construction materials that would usually end up in landfills and re-sells them. Hawaii also has a new law that 'electronics must be recycled by the manufacturer'. Participants are encouraged to think how they could "close the loop" on linear processes or relationships in their homes and workplaces.

PRINCIPLE 3: ECOLOGICAL/CARBON FOOTPRINT

These both describe how much of nature your lifestyle requires. Methods and websites for calculating the footprints for individuals, organizations, and businesses are shared, including a discussion of their usefulness as metrics as well as their limitations. Footprints of developed vs. developing are compared and the class discusses and learns what contributes to large footprints and what actions minimize them. Carbon taxing and cap and trade are introduced as policies that would provide incentives for widespread, large-scale footprint reduction. Case studies include Evolution Sage, a Hawaii based non-profit that provides local carbon offsetting; Hagadone Printing, Hawaii's only printing company that off-sets all of its carbon production; and the greenhouse gas inventory at UHM, as well as many Sustainable Saunders projects.

PRINCIPLE 4: ZERO WASTE

Principle 4 introduces the concept of producing no waste through recycling, composting, repurposing, and reducing. Toronto, Canada, with its curbside compost pick-up and unsorted curbside recycling pick-up, is used as an example of "closing the loop" for Zero Waste. Humboldt County in California also provides enough energy from their municipal compost facility to fuel their entire wastewater treatment plant.

Sustainable Saunders dumpster dive waste audits and efforts for a plastic-free campus, including implementing bio-compostables and tray-less cafeterias to reduce plate waste and water use, demonstrate 'reducing your footprint' for Zero Waste.

PRINCIPLE 5: ZERO ENERGY

Zero Energy is the concept of buildings and campuses producing more energy than they consume, receiving an energy paycheck rather than an energy bill. This module demonstrates the little-known difference between conservation and efficiency. It shows the role of renewable energy and basic policies and financial models that make its implementation viable. Peak energy shaving and the role of electric cars are explored. The Sustainable Saunders energy audit and survey for Saunders Hall and Hamilton Library including our CFL swap out, de-lamping, air-conditioning shut-downs and measurement of occupant health and happiness are all included as examples.

Principle 6: Local First

'Local first' is introduced in terms of food miles and multiplier effects for healthy local economies. Reasons for local first include reducing carbon footprint, healthier food, and resiliency of your community. Global trends toward local first are described, including the case study of local currency in Salt Spring Island, Canada. Campus case studies include building relationships with local vendors and farmers for food and services.

Principle 7: Carrying Capacity and Self-Sufficiency

These terms are defined as the ability to be self-sufficient as a region, which has magnified importance for Hawaii as the most remote population center on earth. Hawaii's dependence on imported fossil fuel, food, services and goods is thoroughly discussed. The *ahupua'a* is re-introduced as a unique model that inspires many of the HUB and people throughout Hawaii. It is the way ancient Hawaiians divided the islands into pie shaped wedges, each of which ran from the mountain to the sea. It is difficult to briefly describe the *ahupua'a* since it is incredibly deep in cultural meaning and history. Each wedge, or *ahupua'a*, was self-governed and self-sustaining, thus honored its self-carrying capacity with amazingly intricate methods of cultivating land and aquaculture. A population similar to that in Hawaii today was able to be completely self-sufficient in every way with resources at every elevation within each district. It is a model that inspires us in Hawaii, but can also serve as a great inspiration for the world.

ENDNOTES

1. http://wordnet.princeton.edu/sustain
2. http://wordnet.princeton.edu/sustainability
3. http://wordnet.princeton.edu/evolve
4. http://wordnet. princeton.edu/evolution
5. http://www.thefreedictionary.com/emerge
6. http://www.thefreedictionary.com/transformation

Methodology for Educational Sustainability Assessments

During a sixteen-week period between March 8, 2010, and June 25, 2010, a group of six University of Hawaii interns, referred to as the Ewa Green Crew (EGC), worked collectively to gather data for energy, waste and water savings at a K-6 school in Ewa Beach, Hawaii. We call this an 'Educational Sustainability Assessment' rather than an audit to so as not confuse what we do with what those in industry do. Our process is intended to be an experiential education for the participants and building occupants while also identifying opportunities for resource savings.

This section outlines the crew's methodology, which is modeled after the Sustainable Saunders initiative at the University of Hawaii at Manoa (UHM). Assessments at Saunders Hall at UHM resulted in changes that reduced a significant amount of unnecessary energy and waste consumption, saving the building $150,000 annually. Using the same methodology, the organization Sustainable UH found opportunities for significant savings at the US Coast Guard Sand Island Base, as well as at other buildings on the UHM campus including the Richardson Law School and Hamilton Library.

This methodology provides a brief description of how to perform simple educational assessments for energy, waste and water including:

- survey
- lighting
- air conditioning
- plug load
- waste
- water
- Energy Star rating

For the full report please visit:
http://sustainable.hawaii.edu/reports.html

METHOD OF DISTRIBUTING SURVEYS

The Comfort Survey assessed the baseline comfort level for the occupants of the elementary school. In order to assess the occupants' comfort including temperature, air quality, lighting, and recycling, the survey was sent out to all members of the school including faculty, staff, teachers, and students.

The survey was distributed in hard copy in two different formats: adult comfort assessment and student comfort assessment. Survey questions were compiled by the members of the EGC, and were tightly based on the template of the Baseline Comfort Survey compiled by members of the Sustainable Saunders student group and included feedback from UHM faculty and staff from many disciplines including statistics, engineering, law, and public policy. The student survey consisted of five short questions and was an abbreviated version of the questions in the adult survey. Both surveys included the same aspects of concern.

The surveys that were distributed to the members of the school on paper that resulted in 100% participation were later entered into an online surveying site, Surveymonkey, for automated analysis.

Here is an example list of a Sustainability Assessment Comfort Survey:

Introduction:

Thanks for participating in this survey that will be used to improve comfort while simultaneously improving facilities. On behalf of your Principal and Facilities department, Sustainable UH has compiled these questions to assess your perception of room temperature comfort, lighting, recycling, and transportation facilities. The survey will only take 5-10 minutes to complete. All the questions are 'select only one answer' unless specified. There are a total of 24 short questions and a comment section at the end of the survey.

Mahalo! (thank you in Hawaiian)

1. Please indicate your position classification:
   - ☐ Faculty
   - ☐ Staff
   - ☐ Administration
   - ☐ Student hire working less than 10 hr per week
   - ☐ Student hire working more than 10 hr per week
   - ☐ Student

2. List your room number (employees only: please complete this survey for your work space).

3. How often are you in your workspace on weekends? (This question determines if buildings can be shut down on weekends, or are perhaps being kept in full operation for just one or a few people.)
   - ☐ Every weekend
   - ☐ Every other weekend
   - ☐ Once a month
   - ☐ Never
   - ☐ Other (please specify)_____

4. Please specify all work hour time slots you are in your workspace during a typical workweek. Please note any exceptions to this schedule: (This question determines if a building can be shut down during certain hours when not in use.)

   [schedule matrix]

5. Do you typically turn on the air conditioning in your work area?

   ☐ Yes

   ☐ No

   ☐ I cannot control the air conditioning in my work area

   ☐ Other_____

6. When do you typically turn off the air conditioning in your work area?

   ☐ When it's too cold

   ☐ At the end of the day

   ☐ At lunch

   ☐ If it is too noisy

   ☐ I cannot control the air conditioning in my work area

7. Do you use any of the following to control the temperature in your workspace:

   ☐ Heater

   ☐ Humidifier

   ☐ Dehumidifier

   ☐ Fan

   ☐ None of the above

   ☐ Other _____

8. How far would you have to move your desk to be directly under the nearest overhead light source? (Illumination

measurements can be taken where desks are most often positioned. In Saunders Hall the rooms were lit so that even the far corners were to lighting standards, yet most desks were under the fixtures and experienced lighting levels three times higher than healthy levels.)

- ☐ I wouldn't have to move, the light is directly over my desk
- ☐ Less than six inches
- ☐ One foot
- ☐ Two feet
- ☐ Three feet
- ☐ Four feet
- ☐ Five feet
- ☐ More than five feet

9. Do you use any of the following to light your workspace IN ADDITION TO the ceiling lights?
    - ☐ Desk lamp
    - ☐ Natural day lighting through the windows
    - ☐ Floor lamp
    - ☐ None of the above

10. Do you use any of the following to light your workspace INSTEAD OF the ceiling lights?
    - ☐ Desk lamp
    - ☐ Natural day lighting through the windows
    - ☐ Floor lamp
    - ☐ None of the above

11. Do you have control over your lights? If not, skip to question [14]
    - ☐ Yes
    - ☐ No

12. During the hours you have spent in your office, would you:

☐ Never or almost never turn on the lights

☐ Always or almost always turn on the lights

☐ Partially or sometimes turn on the lights

☐ Please explain_____

_____

13. Do you typically turn OFF your lights when you leave your workspace?

☐ Yes

☐ No

☐ Not if others are using or will shortly be using the workspace

☐ I try but I sometimes forget

☐ Other

☐ Please explain_____

14. The following describes my experience with the lighting in my workspace:

☐ Very over lit

☐ Somewhat over lit

☐ Just right

☐ Somewhat dim

☐ Very dim

15. Please check any of the following symptoms you have experienced in your workspace: (Ask this question again after lighting is brought into healthy levels to gauge the improvement.)

☐ Eyestrain

☐ Headache

☐ Stress

☐ Fatigue

☐ No symptoms experienced

☐ Other

☐ Please specify _____

16. The following phrase describes my satisfaction about the room temperature in my workspace:

☐ Much too cold

☐ A bit too cold

☐ The temperature is just right

☐ A bit too warm

☐ Much too warm

17. In your workspace, do you control the:

☐ Fan

☐ Temperature

☐ Fan and temperature

☐ I cannot control the temperature

18. Do you see or smell mold anywhere in your workspace? (i.e. windowsills, surfaces, air vents, etc.)

☐ No

☐ Yes

☐ Where?_____

19. Do you experience allergic or physical reactions while in your workspace? (i.e. stuffy nose, runny nose, coughing, sneezing)

☐ Yes

☐ No

20. Do you recycle at school?
   - ☐ Daily
   - ☐ Often
   - ☐ Sometimes
   - ☐ Never
   - ☐ I was not aware of recycling options

21. Is recycling available in *your* building?
   - ☐ No
   - ☐ Yes

22. Is the recycling convenient for you?
   - ☐ No
   - ☐ Yes

23. How do you usually get to school?
   - ☐ Drive alone
   - ☐ Carpool
   - ☐ Public Transit
   - ☐ Bicycle
   - ☐ Walk
   - ☐ Moped
   - ☐ Skate
   - ☐ Other _____

24. How many miles is your one-way commute to school?

25. How many minutes is your one-way commute to school? (This allows an analysis of how long different modes of transportation take, often dispelling the perception that driving is quicker than biking, for example.)

If there is anything that you think will supplement our study, (i.e. the brightness of the hallways or the temperature of the water in the restrooms, etc.) please feel free to leave a comment, as it will also help improve our workplace.

_____

_____

_____

_____

METHOD OF CONDUCTING LIGHTING ASSESSMENT

The EGC used building floor plans provided by the Department of Education. They pre-drew the shape of each room, the cardinal directions and the placement of doors and windows to identify opportunities for natural day lighting.

During the lighting assessment, the number of lamp fixtures and the number of lamps in each fixture were counted. If there were discrepancies from the floor plans, which often happens, the drawings were updated. Note: the building efficiency industry calls light bulbs lamps, and would consider a bulb something you plant in the ground.

For each different fixture type, a single fixture was taken apart and observed for the number of ballasts it contained. Ballast is a device that feeds and regulates electricity to the lamps. Old ballasts were magnetic and used a lot of electricity, while more modern electric ballasts use an almost negligible amount. We called the ballast manufacturer to identify the type of each ballast, and also to ask if removing one lamp from a ballast would cause a proportional decrease in energy use. For some types of ballast, if you remove a lamp they still use just as much electricity, so it pays to be sure de-lamping efforts will actually result in energy savings.

All similar fixtures were assumed to be the same in terms of ballast type, number of ballasts, and number of lamps. The following were easily read directly from each lamp and were also assumed to be the same for all similar fixtures: lamp length, lamp technology type such as T12 or more efficient T8, and lamp watt usage.

Using a Lutron LX-1010b light meter, two lighting illumination measurements were taken in each room: one at the most lit part of the room and one at the least lit part of the room (at the same task-level such as at desk tops). The same measurements were taken with the lights off to measure natural day lighting and lighting from other rooms. These were subtracted from the original measurements to determine the amount of light from the lamps only. Lamps were removed from rooms that were over-lit until the lighting levels at all task locations was brought to healthy levels as specified by the Illuminating Engineering Society (IES). We also discovered that if the windows were left unobstructed, as shown for room F205 in Fig.9 below, that the natural day lighting would be sufficient for the room.

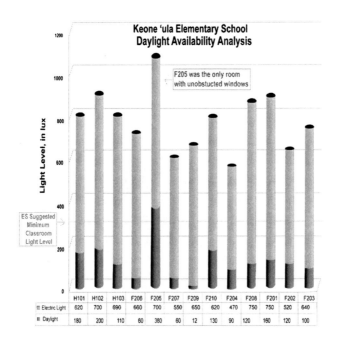

Method of Conducting Air Conditioning Assessment

Temperature Gun Readings

Using a RYOBI™ temperature gun, EGC measured room temperatures of four rooms in each building. Rooms best facing north, east, south, and west were selected to determine if heat gain from the sun affected the room temperature.

Temperature readings were recorded in 30-minute intervals. All classroom readings were taken on the same type of light brown laminate desk surface that would have the same thermal properties. Auditors held the temperature gun within one-foot of the surface, using the same location for each room's subsequent data recording to ensure consistency and accuracy. Temperature readings were also taken at the teacher's desk surface or, in the absence of a teacher's desk, on a surface most frequently used by occupants. In addition, the thermostat temperature in each room was recorded. Temperature readings were also taken at the vent where air-conditioned air entered the vent, which could be fairly compared between rooms.

Rooms that do not have air conditioning were used as a control to observe temperature fluctuations throughout the day. They showed the heat gain from the sun when no air conditioning was present over the course of a day.

In addition to temperature profiles, the EGC created scatterplot diagrams to show a snapshot of the temperatures in all rooms based on the temperature gun readings taken between 2:00 and 2:30 pm. The scatterplot diagrams provided a comparison of room temperatures throughout the School at a particular time.

Data Logging buttons

Based on the scatterplot diagrams and the temperature gun readings, four rooms were selected for temperature measurement throughout a 24-hour period. The team used small wireless data loggers made by Onset Computer Corporation called HOBO buttons that take readings of temperature, humidity and light illumination every minute (Thumann, Younger, & Niehus, 2010, p. 90). With the data downloaded and plotted on a graph, we could easily see when the rooms were being overly air conditioned.

We also plotted the outside air temperature on the same graph and drew a horizontal line at the ideal temperature of 76 degrees for tropical weather, which for non-tropical climates is set even higher at 78 degrees (Thumann, Younger, & Niehus, 2010, p. 216). By comparing the areas above and below the ideal temperature line, we were able to calculate the percentage of excess air conditioning. This revealed a savings of 53% that enabled us to show the thousands of dollars that would be saved every month if the air conditioning was brought into healthy levels.

METHOD OF CONDUCTING PLUGLOAD ASSESSMENT

A P4400 Kill-A-Watt electric usage monitor was used to measure phantom loads, watts drawn while appliances and electronic devices were plugged in and not in use or turned off.

During the assessment, the number of electronic devices that were plugged in was counted and the amount of watts each used was recorded. This could be found written on plates mounted on the device, by looking up the model on the Internet or calling the manufacturer. From the data collected, the cost to power those devices in phantom load for a whole year was calculated to determine how much could be saved if they were unplugged when not in use. A simple way to do this is to place the appliances on power strips that are turned off when not in use. Some power strips have occupancy sensors that will switch off when no one is in the room. Smart strips have one control plug that senses a drop in electricity use and turns off all other items plugged into the strip. For example, you could plug your computer into the control socket and when you turn your computer off, your printer, desk lamp and any other items plugged into the strip would also switch off.

Method of Conducting Waste Assessment

The total amount of garbage was divided into thirds, and each carefully analyzed as a sample of the whole amount of waste collected over a 24-hour period. After sorting out the waste, the daily output was used to find weekly and monthly data on what was being thrown away and the amount spent on waste management.

A series of 18-gallon Rubbermaid bins were lined with garbage bags. As the team sorted the trash, each bin was filled with a certain type of refuse such as non-recyclable plastic. After the bins were filled, the bags were pulled out and weighed on a bathroom scale. The auditors first weighed themselves, then weighed themselves holding the bag of trash and recorded the difference. The categories of refuse included the following:

> Milk Cartons
>
> Green Waste
>
> Styrofoam trays
>
> Recyclable Metal and Plastic
>
> White Paper and Cardboard
>
> Non-recyclable plastic
>
> Other Trash

Trash was sorted, measured by volume and weight, and re-bagged. It was disgusting. By identifying categories of waste that could be recycled or composted, the excess amount of money that was spent on transport to the landfill as well as dumping fees could be calculated to justify any expenditures needed to implement waste management programs.

Method of Conducting a Water Assessment

According to research published in *Pediatrics for Medical Students* 2nd Edition (Bernstein & Shelov, 2002) the average amount of daily trips to the restroom for 30kg 9 year olds is 2.8 times per student. The average number of times a student must defecate

daily is one. Combining these values with the gallons/flush specified on each toilet and urinal yielded a rough estimate for annual
water flushing at 1,033,332 gallons. This comes out to $3,084 a
year based on a water fee of $2.98/gallon. Sewage fees are higher
than actual water fees, and this school pays a flat sewage fee based
on the number of students, teachers and faculty. Changing water
usage would not change the sewage fee in this case.

By using low flow toilets and urinals, a considerable amount
of water use can be reduced. The Sustainable Saunders initiative
calculated that replacing every urinal and toilet in the bathrooms
would have a ten year payback period, meaning it would take
around ten years to recoup the cost through water savings. Interestingly, using laser counters above each urinal in one bathroom
revealed that nearly 80% of visitors use the first stall. By replacing
just the first urinal or toilet encountered, 80% of the water savings would be realized and the payback period would be reduced
to a very reasonable 3.75 years.

Aerators are tiny screens placed in faucets to reduce water
flow. In the case of KES, they provide 1.6 gpm. A tap designed
to eliminate faucets that are left on must be pressed and held for
water to flow. This can provide considerable cost reduction. The
Sustainable Saunders initiative found that taps are anecdotally left
on once per week in a bathroom, wasting a lot of water. Assuming each child uses the tap for 5 seconds for each bathroom
visit, it was estimated that 380 gallons are used daily and 138,515
gallons annually for sink use.

Combining urinal, toilet, and sink water usage, the school
used 4,685 gallons per day and 1,171,850 gallons per year for
their bathrooms. Removing this amount from the total water
bill leaves 14,818,150 gallons of water that is most probably used
for irrigation. An assessment of leaks in the irrigation system,
as well as identifying the opportunity to use sink water, known
as greywater, and rainwater catchment to irrigate, would have a
considerable impact on reducing the school's water bill.

Method for Collecting Data for Energy Star Savings

Data necessary to begin benchmarking with ENERGY STAR can be collected by anyone and entered into the online portfolio manager program upon free registration. This includes the following information for each building:

1. Physical location (address)

2. Year built

3. Total Square footage of usable space (not including walls and partitions, but also including parking areas, covered lanais and swimming pools)

4. Percentage of the building that is cooled using AC

5. Percentage of the building that is heated

6. Number of computer monitors

7. Number of occupants

8. Operational hours

9. Number of walk-in freezers (for k-12 and warehouse spaces only)

For accurate data collection, the best method is to use the building drawing plans and confirm with a walk-through of the site. A copy of the architectural drawing plans will usually provide the square footage of the building as well as other important physical aspects such as how many floors, rooms and halls the building has, as well as the physical location and year built. The most recent edition of floor plans that include any new additions can be used to calculate the square footage including parking structures, covered lanais and swimming pools. Plans will usually include total square footage with net usable space and the mechanical and electrical layout where the number of lighting fixtures and the ventilation units can be counted.

Methods for finding the square footage for the building include using survey tools to physically measure the total area on-site or using digital methods. Various computer programs such as BMI can also provide accurate calculations. Although a lot of information can be obtained from the building plans and/or digital sources, it is important to do a building walk-through to check for any additions or alterations that may have been made to the building. For gathering other information such as the number of computer monitors, walk-in freezers or persons in the building and the percentage of the buildings that is cooled or heated, the best method is to make an on-site visit. While on location the auditor can count, record, and cross-check pertinent information.

METHOD OF EDUCATIONAL OUTREACH

To help increase awareness of sustainability at the elementary school, the EGC set up displays at their school library for students, teachers and staff to view during the month leading up to Earth Day. One display covered the topic of energy consumption, while the other display included information about waste on the island of Oahu. On Earth Day the EGC hosted classes from kindergarten to grade six in an interactive workshop with the displays.

Energy Display

The purpose of the energy display was to show how energy can be wasted in homes and how easy it can be to save money and reduce the use of energy. The first energy poster displayed three different types of light bulbs: a CFL, an incandescent, and a LED. In order to put this in a quantitative analogy that students could relate to, candy bars were used to demonstrate the amount of potential energy that could be saved. Comparing the three different types of light bulbs showed that the incandescent light used 60 watts, the CFL used 13-15 watts (60% less than an incandescent), and the LED used just 6-8 watts (85% less than an incandescent). Using this information, the poster showed how many candy bars a student could purchase with extra money from energy savings. Assuming that one candy bar is equal to one dollar, with the energy savings students could buy 0 candy bars with an incandescent bulb, 8 candy bars with a CFL, and 10 candy bars with a LED.

'Energy Vampire,' the second energy poster, depicted a cartoon vampire surrounded by lightning that aimed to educate the students about phantom loads. Phantom load is a term used to describe the energy lost in homes when appliances are plugged in to outlets while not in use. A plugged-in appliance consumes energy even when turned off. The vampire was standing on a real power strip with common electrical appliances such as a cell phone charger, a fan, a toaster and a play station plugged into it. During the presentation a kilowatt reader showed the amount of energy used when things are plugged in to the power strip but not turned on. The lesson behind this display was that just having the appliances plugged into the power strip is not enough. In order to reduce the phantom load and save energy the power strip must be turned off.

Waste Display

The second Earth Day display was about waste and recycling. The purpose of the display was to show how much garbage is thrown away and how much of that amount could be diverted from the landfill. The EGC team set up a display consisting of bags of garbage representing the total percentage of each category as shown:

Total Paper	30.2%
Total Plastic	12.1%
Total Metals	4.8%
Total Glass	1.7%
Total Other Inorganic	3.1%
Total Other Waste	9.8%
Total Green Waste	8.7%
Total Wood	4.5%
Total Other Organics	24.80%

Fig. 12: Oahu's Landfill composition (www.opala.org)

Based on the Fig. 12, over 80% of the total garbage that goes out each week can be diverted from the landfill. The display showed what types of things go into each category, what can be and should be recycled and what goes into the landfill.

The side of the display titled 'Eco-cycle' showed what can be recycled and the processes it goes through including composting, making dirt fertilizer for gardens, or remaking plastic and glass products like beverage bottles into new products like clothing and playground equipment.

On the non-recyclable or 'One-way Ticket to the Landfill' side, there was less than 15 % of the overall garbage and that included trash in the form of Styrofoam containers, rubber slippers, aerosol cans and other types of non-recyclable garbage.

Teachers brought their classes to view these displays in the library over the weeks leading up to Earth Day. Then on Earth Day, the KES team hosted classes for an interactive presentation of the displays. The Earth Day displays earned a positive response for the EGC team. The students were engaged and asked insightful questions during the presentation. This was a great way to conceptualize ideas of sustainability in a way that children understood. In addition, we were able to dispel an unexpected opinion on where our electricity comes from. The most popular answer had been that the sockets in our walls were powered by lightning.

Bibliography

2050, H. (2008). *Hawaii 2050 Task Force on Sustainability Report.* Public Policy Center, Honolulu.

Agency, E. P. (2010, April). *Climate Change and Society.* Retrieved April 28, 2010, from EPA Climate Change: http://www.epa.gov/climatechange/downloads/Climate_Change_Society.pdf

Arnstein, S. R. (1969). A Ladder of Citizen Participation. *Journal of the American Planning Association,* Vol 35, No 4, 216-224.

Berke, P., & Conroy, M. M. (2000). Are We Planning for Sustainable Development? *Journal of the American Planning Association,* Vol 66, No 1, 21-33.

Bollmeier, W., Loudat, T., & Kasturi, P. (2003). *Interim Report On Renewables and Unconventional Energy in Hawaii.* University of Hawaii at Manoa, Hawaii Energy Policy Project, Honolulu.

Buckingham, Marcus, & Clifton, Donald O. (2001). *Now Discover Your Strengths,* New York: Simon & Schuster (The Free Press).

Callahan, G., & Ikeda, S. 2004. The Career of Robert Moses, City Planning as a Microcosm of Socialism. *The Independent Review,* Vol IX, No 2, 253-261.

Campbell, S. (1996). Green Cities, Growing Cities, Just Cities? Urban Planning and the Contradictions of Sustainable Development. *Journal of the American Planning Association,* Vol 62, 296-312.

Choi, F. (2007). Analyses of Economic, Environmental, and Occupant Benefits of Sustainable Design and LEED Certificaiton for State of Hawaii Public School Facilities. In R. B. Lincolne Scott (Ed.), *Hawaii Green Building Conference. May 9*. Honolulu: DBEDT.

Christensen, K. S. (1985). Coping with Uncertainty in Planning. *Journal of American Planning Association,* Vol 43, 341-345.

Coffman, M., & Umemoto, K. (2009). Back to the Roots of Sustainability Planning. Available from the UHM Department of Urban and Regional Planning.

Cooney, S. (2009). *Build a Green Small Business: Profitable Ways to Become an Ecopreneur.* New York: McGraw-Hill.

Csikszentmihalyi, M. (1990). *Flow: The Psychology of Optimal Experience.* New York: Harper and Row.

Dator, J. (2006, June 29). *Dator's "Laws" of the Futures (and of Futures Studies).* Retrieved April 25, 2010, from Futures Studies: http://www.futures.hawaii.edu/2006/06/jamais-12-jims-7.php

Dator, J. (1999, February). From Tsunamis to Long Waves and Back. *Futures,* Vol 31, No 1, 1-23.

Dator, J. (1998, November). The Future Lies Behind! *American Behavioral Scientist,* Vol 42, No 3, 1-12.

Dator, J. (2009). The Unholy Trinity, Plus One. *Journal of Futures Studies, 13(3),* 33-48.

Development, T. W. (1987). *Our Common Future.* Oxford: Oxford University Press.

Electric, H. (2008). *Hawaiian Electric 2008 Sustainability Report.* Retrieved April 25, 2010, from http://www.heco.com/vcmcontent/StaticFiles/pdf/Sustainable_ARvf1_2009.pdf

Energy, Dept. of (2010). Retrieved from http://www.energy.gov/applianceselectronics.htm

Environmental Protection Agency (2010, April). *Climate Change and Society.* Retrieved April 28, 2010, from EPA Climate Change: http://www.epa.gov/climatechange/downloads/Climate_Change_Society.pdf

Fisher, R. (1977). *Urban Utopias: Ebenezer Howard, Frank Lloyd Wright and Le Corbusier.* Cambridge: Blackwell Publishers.

Graefe, L. (2009). The Peak Oil Debate. *Economic Review,* Vol 94, No 2, 1-13.

Gunder, M. (2006). Sustainability: Planning's Saving Grace or Road to Perdition. *Journal of Planning, Education and Research,* Vol 26, No 2, 208-221.

Hall, P. (1999). The City of Enterprise. *Cities of Tomorrow* (p. 383). Oxford, UK: Blackwell Publishers.

Hardin, G. (1968). The Tragedy of the Commons. *Science, 162,* 1243-1248.

Hawken, P. (1994). *The Ecology of Commerce.* New York: HarperCollins.

Hawken, P. (2007). *Blessed Unrest: How the Largest Movement in the World Came into Being and Why No One Saw it Coming.* New York: Viking.

Heschong, L. (2002, June). Daylighting and Human Performance. *ASHRAE Journal,* Vol 44, No 6, 65-67.

Huston, J. (1998). Maximizing Evolvability. *American Behavioral Scientist,* Vol 42, No 3, 436-439.

Initiative, H. C. (2008). *Agreement Among the State of Hawaii, Division of Consumer Advocacy of the Department of Commerce and*

Consumer Affairs, and Hawaiian Electric Companies. Honolulu.

Innes, J. (1992). Group Process and Social Construction of Growth Management. *Journal of the American Planning Association,* Vol 58, 440-451.

Jacobs, J. (1961). The Death and Life of Great American Cities. In S. Campbell, & S. Feinstein, *Reading in Planning Theory* (Chapter 4). Cambridge, Mass: Blackwell.

Kelly, L., Cashore, B., Bernstein, S., & Auld, G. (2009). Paying it Forward: Path Dependency, Progressive Incrementalism, and the "Super Wicked" Problem of Global Climate Change. *Climate Change: Global Risks, Challenges and Decisions, March 10-12.* Copenhagen, Denmark.

Klein, J. (1990). *Interdisciplinarity: History, Theory, and Practice.* Wayne State: Wayne State University Press.

Kloosterman, K. (2010, June 28). *Israelis and Palestinians collaborate in wind energy.* Retrieved November 15, 2010, from Ministry of Foreign Affairs - the State of Israel: http://www.mfa.gov.il/MFA/Israel+beyond+politics/Israelis_Palestinians_collaborate_wind_energy_28-Jun-2010

Krisberg, K. (2009). Future of energy, a growing interest for public health field: Health impact of dwindling oil supplies. *The Nation's Health,* Vol 39, No 6, 1-8.

McFarland, E., Hunt, J., & Campbell, J. (2001). *Energy, Physics and the Environment.* Guelph, Ontario, Canada: Thomson Learning Custom Publishing.

McKenzie-Mohr, D. (2006). *Fostering Sustainable Behavior.* Retrieved April 25, 2010, from Community Based Social Marketing: www.cbsm.com

Montessori, M. (1912). *The Montessori Method.* Retrieved April 15, 2010, from Montessori 101: http://www.montessori. org/sitefiles/Montessori_101_nonprintable.pdf

Nations, U. (1972). *Report of the United Nations Conference on the Human Environment.* Stockholm: United Nations Publications.

Nations, U. (1972, June 16). *United Nations Environment Programme.* Retrieved April 25, 2010, from http://www.unep. org/Documents.Multilingual/Default.Print.asp?document id=97&articleid=1503

North, J. (2010). *The Total Economic Impact of Faronics Power Save.* Cambridge: Forester Consulting.

Paidipati, J., Sawyer, H., & Kurrasch, A. (2008, Feb.). *Rooftop Photovoltaics Market Penetration Scenarios.* (NREL, Producer) Retrieved April 10, 2010, from http://www1.eere.energy. gov/solar/solar_america/pdfs/42306.pdf

Rocha, E. (1997). Ladder of Empowerment. *Journal of Planning Education and Research,* Vol 17, No 1, 31-44.

Rome, Club of (1972). Retrieved 2008, from http://www. clubofrome.org/about/methodology.php.

Sandercock, L. (1998). The Difference that Theory Makes. In L. Sandercock, *Towards Cosmopolis: Planning for Multicultural Cities.* West Sussex: John Wiley & Sons.

Solarbuzz. (2010). Retrieved from www.solarbuzz.com

Thumann, A., Younger, W., & Niehus, T. (2010). *Handbook of Energy Audits,* 8th Ed. Lilburn, GA: The Fairmont Press, Inc.

Willard, B. 2002. *The Sustainability Advantage: Seven Business Case Benefits of a Triple Bottom Line.* Gabriola Island, BC, Canada: New Society Publishers.

Wolfe, M. (2008). *Workplace De-Lamping.* University of Hawaii, Public Policy Center. Honolulu: http://www.publicpolicycenter.hawaii.edu/documents/brief004.pdf.

Wustenhagen, R. (2004). Green Energy Market Development in Germany: Effective Public Policy and Emerging Customer Demand. *Institute for Economy and the Environment.*

Yanarella, E. J., & Levine, R. S. (1992, Oct.). Does Sustainable Development Lead to Sustainability? *Futures,* 759-774.

Yandle, B., Vijayaraghavan, M., & Bhattarai, M. (2002, May). The Environmental Kuznets Curve, A Primer. *PERC Research Study,* 1-24.

About the Author

Shanah Faith Trevenna is the Coordinator of Sustainable UH, a campus organization that is working to establish the University of Hawaii (UH) System as one of the world leaders in sustainability. She coordinated a dynamic interdisciplinary student team called the HUB (Help Us Bridge) that implemented many no-to-low-cost projects for water, waste and energy management adding up to hundreds of thousands of dollars in annual savings for the university. She used their lessons learned to design 'Sustainability 101', a curriculum that has been taught throughout the UH system, as well as the Department of Education in Hawaii.

She holds a degree in Mechanical Engineering from the University of Western Ontario in Canada and a Masters Degree in Urban Planning from the University of Hawaii. She merges a decade of experience working for corporations such as IBM and Philips as well as local engineering firms in Hawaii, with a passion for grassroots community empowerment. She was honored with the 2008 UH Presidential 'Making the Elephants Dance' award for finding creative ways for the University to be responsive to the community's needs. In 2009, Hawaii Business Magazine named her one of five that will shape Hawaii for the next 50 years. The American College Professional Association

(ACPA) named her their 2010 National Sustainability Champion. As a keynote speaker for national conferences such as ACPA's Harvard Sustainability Institute, she strives to share UH's success with the nation and beyond.

Shanah currently lives in Hawaii. She teaches an honors course on sustainability and internships at the University of Hawaii. She is pursuing her PhD in Political Science, is the President of the Sustainability Association of Hawaii, is a founding member of Women in Renewable Energy (WIRE), is the Director of the Rewarding Internship for Sustainable Employment (RISE) program, and is the Hawaii Education Consultant for Johnson Controls Inc.

Please visit her web page at: www.SurfingTsunamisOfChange.com

Reviews for Tsunamis of Change

"The world is in need of change right now, and it takes a special lens to view change as an opportunity to not only do well, but to do good.

"Shanah Trevenna has a passion and a talent for sharing this new worldview that sustainability requires. The story these spirited change agents share include concrete principles and tools that will empower the reader to believe that championing change is not only entirely possible, it's already happening today."

—Ray C. Anderson, founder and chairman, Interface, Inc., TIME Magazine's Greenest CEO, and author, *Mid-Course Correction and Business Lessons from a Radical Industrialist*

"Concepts such as peak oil, peak water, and climate change point to the idea that the global economy is at a crossroads. To assure that future generations can prevent health epidemics, the displacement of millions of climate refugees, and wars over ever-dwindling resources, our choice at this crossroad is painfully clear. Building a sustainable, green economy that is fair and equitable is our generation's moral imperative. The good news is that not only is this possible, but it is happening everywhere, and it is happening at a pace that may make sustainability a global economic driver on par with the Industrial Revolution.

"Shanah Trevenna brings the productivity of her engineer's mindset to lay out practical, tangible solutions that create win-win scenarios for all stakeholders: environmental, economic, and social. Readers will learn to catch the wave and join the most exciting sea change in modern times...and leave naysayers behind as obsolete relics of the old economy."

—Scott Cooney, Founder and Principal of GreenBusinessOwner.com, and author of *Build a Green Small Business: Profitable Ways to Become an Ecopreneur* (McGraw-Hill)

"This new book shows us that becoming more sustainable is like learning to surf—difficult and awkward at first, but then fun and inspiring. With her motto "Sustainability is sexy," Shanah Trevenna offers personal tips and practical insights about how to ride these waves of change with courage and grace. Just as surfing is about finding your balance and going with the flow of nature, the author shows us a balanced and sustainable way of facing both personal and global challenges."

—Stuart H. Coleman, Hawaii Coordinator of the Surfrider Foundation and author of *Eddie Would Go* and *Fierce Heart*

"This book can be read as a narrative, a memoir, or as a case study; however, as the title suggests, it is really handbook for creating positive change in any arena. It can be read as a book about sustainability, or as a guide to cultivating leaders and the change agent skills they will bring to the future. These skills, articulated by College Student Educators International (ACPA) include: resiliency, curiosity, passion, self-awareness, tenaciousness, assertiveness, empathy, and optimism, among others."

—Krista Hiser, Associate Professor of English, KCC – University of Hawaii

"Perhaps it was what [Professor] Dator referred to as Trevenna's 'mastery of facts ... and uncanny ability to mobilize people,' as well as her tenacity in getting the task accomplished that eventually prevailed over skepticism. Lucky for UH, and Hawai'i, Trevenna was undeterred, setting about to make her case: Hawai'i has the potential to be the global leader in both food and energy sustainability."

—KaLeo, The Voice, University of Hawaii, Manoa.

Breinigsville, PA USA
14 February 2011
255484BV00002B/4/P